Saving Women from the Church

How Jesus Mends a Divide

by Susan McLeod-Harrison

BARCLAY PRESS
Newberg, OR 97132

SAVING WOMEN FROM THE CHURCH

How Jesus Mends a Divide

© 2008 by Susan McLeod-Harrison

Published by
BARCLAY PRESS
211 N. Meridian St., #101
Newberg, OR 97132
800.962.4014
www.barclaypress.com

ISBN 978-1-59498-013-8

All rights reserved.
No part of this publication may be reproduced,
stored in a retrieval system, or transmitted in
any form or by any means—for example, electronic,
photocopy, recording—without the prior
written permission of the publisher.
The only exception is brief quotations
in printed reviews.

All Scripture quotations, unless otherwise indicated, are taken
from the *Holy Bible, Today's New International Version®. TNIV®*.
Copyright © 2002, 2004 by International Bible Society.
Used by permission of Zondervan. All rights reserved.

Scripture quotations marked *NRSV* are taken from the
New Revised Standard Version Bible, copyright 1989,
Division of Christian Education of the National Council
of Churches of Christ in the United States of America.
Used by permission. All rights reserved.

Cover design by Darryl Brown

Can we be honest? Here are the hard questions that real women ask. There are no easy answers. So where do we go with these questions? The book directs us to Jesus. Not a hackneyed, familiar Jesus, but a person so fresh I never would have imagined him this way.

Miriam Adeney

associate professor of global and urban ministries, Seattle Pacific University; teaching fellow, Regent College; adjunct professor, Fuller Theological Seminary

The church is long overdue for another Reformation, and Susan McLeod-Harrison is leading the way. Why has the church relegated women to the back bench for so long? Why have men and women of good will tolerated it? For too many years, the Bible has been used as a weapon to denigrate and diminish our sisters. With solid exegesis and prophetic prose, Susan helps us see Jesus, ourselves, and the church with fresh eyes. This book is long overdue.

Philip Gulley

Quaker pastor and writer

In this creative and engaging book, Susan McLeod-Harrison offers a thoughtful, biblical approach to a misunderstood topic. *Saving Women from the Church* provides hope, healing, and insight to any woman with questions about God's view of women.

Elisa Stanford

author of *Ordinary Losses: Naming the Graces that Shape Us* (Paraclete Press, 2004)

This is the book my heart was waiting for. I've needed this book a hundred times—as a young woman trying to discern my place in the church; as a seminary student desperately struggling to reconcile a rigid reading of Scripture with my calling to minister; and as a pastor wanting to somehow create a safe place for women, knowing how the church I loved had too often failed me. *Saving Women from the Church* offers solid biblical scholarship combined with thoughtful and compassionate narrative. The tender and reflective meditations for healing make this an excellent resource for any study group.

Angie Best-Boss

senior pastor, West Newton Friends Meeting;
author of *The Heart of a Shepherd: Devotions for New Pastors* (Judson Press, 2000) and *Surviving Your First Year of Ministry: What Seminary Couldn't Teach You* (Judson Press, 1999)

This very readable book offers genuine hope and guidance. The author writes with wholesome passion, utilizing well the findings and insights of biblical scholars on both the content of the New Testament and on the best methods of interpretation. It seems proper that a book supporting women's rightful place in the church and its ministries comes from a publisher in the Friends (Quaker) Church tradition.

David M. Scholer

Professor of New Testament
Fuller Theological Seminary, Pasadena, California

An easy read and a forthright addition to the world of books on women and the church.

L.L. Barkat

author of *Stone Crossings: Finding Grace in Hard and Hidden Places* (InterVarsity Press, 2008)

To my mother,
Jo Anne Rhudy Harrison;
my mother-in-law,
Jean Phillips McLeod;
and in memory of my grandmother,
Ruby Register Rhudy—all
gifted women who have
served in Jesus' church.

Contents

	Foreword	*xiii*
	Introduction	*1*
chapter 1	If you've felt alienated and judged in church...	*13*
chapter 2	If you've believed women are inferior to men...	*29*
chapter 3	If the church has resisted your call to minister...	*43*
chapter 4	If you've been told that emotional expression is a weakness...	*61*
chapter 5	If church has been an unsafe place to share your woundedness...	*77*
chapter 6	If, as a single woman, your gifts have been rejected or overlooked...	*91*
chapter 7	If you've felt controlled by the misuse of Scriptures on submission...	*107*

chapter 8	If you've heard that women and men shouldn't cominister…	*121*
chapter 9	If you don't have the emotional energy to "succeed" in ministry…	*135*
chapter 10	If you've been encouraged to deify motherhood…	*147*
chapter 11	If you've ever felt your kids aren't welcome…	*159*
chapter 12	If you've felt left alone in your grief and pain…	*171*
	Conclusion	*183*
Appendix A:	Interpreting the Bible (or "Hermeneutics")	*187*
Appendix B:	The Role of Culture in Commands toward Slaves and Women	*193*
Appendix C:	A Brief Look at 1 Timothy 2:8-15	*199*
	Recommended Reading	*209*

Acknowledgments

Because the journey of writing this book started in my youth and ended in my middle age, my "thank-you" list is like revisiting many of the people and communities that have enriched my life so far. That said, I will start with those people who helped me in the book's earliest stages.

Ken Smith taught me creative writing at the University of Tennessee at Chattanooga in the late 1980s. He was the first person outside my family to recognize that I could write. Even though I do not write as well as he taught me, his warm affirmation helped me pick up the proverbial pen with the outrageous idea I had something to say.

Carolyn Lonas and I taught a Sunday school class on Jesus and women in the mid-1990s. At that time, Carolyn would not have agreed with many of the premises of this book, and it may be she still doesn't. Her eager mind and curiosity could not stop her, however, from encouraging me in my own question-asking. Her support in coteaching the class was pivotal, as the healing I received from what I have come to call "Jesus' law of love" was foundational for everything that followed.

Several years later, Cerese Travis read the very embryonic manuscript and wrote encouraging comments. During my Vancouver years, Kathleen Lagore read and encouraged, Christina Chiu graciously edited for me (especially chapter seven), Rick Hiebert provided his writing and editing expertise, and Connie Furr helped with the introduction, especially the need to address the *imago dei*.

In my next stage of life, my husband, Mark McLeod-Harrison, provided immense and unending encouragement, editorial feedback, and gave me the idea for the "Meditations for Healing." It was due to his belief in me and in this project that the book found a publishing home with Barclay Press. Our relatives, Vickie and Megan Malone also provided enthusiastic support after reading the manuscript. Mark's colleagues and our friends Ed Higgins and Kendra Irons read chapters and gave helpful feedback. The late Colleen Richmond, beloved English professor at George Fox University, read through the entire manuscript, edited, and provided encouraging comments. Kate Merriman, who edited a book of my husband's, read a chapter and spurred me to continue with my efforts to find a publisher. Finally, my husband asked his colleague Corey Beals to read a proposal for the book, and Corey passed on the word to Dan McCracken, Barclay Press's publisher, that the book might be right for Barclay. Dan believed in the need for the book and committed to providing the right editor, Liz Heaney. Liz said all the "hard things" that others might have been hesitant to say, and hence, I was able to communicate much more clearly.

After the book was accepted for publication, old friends Jenny Gremm, Shannon Guiboche, Lyn Hallewell, Lisa Jacquemin, Gordie Lagore, Anne-Marie Samarasinghe, Juliana Sutton, and Karen Villalba read chapters and provided edits, comments, and support. Angie McCormick, a new friend, read the entire manuscript and gave extensive, helpful feedback. Thank you also to Maudine Fee, who read the manuscript with an exegetical eye, and to Gordon Fee for reading the introduction and first chapter and giving encouraging feedback. My mom, Jo Anne Harrison, read the manuscript in all its evolutionary stages, and has always supported my efforts to write. Throughout my growing-up years, she provided for me a model of someone who both reads and writes well. Sierra Neiman and Paula Hampton, the editorial staff at Barclay Press, worked hard on the details of the manuscript just before its publication.

Thank you all!

It is likely there are other friends and acquaintances who have read, edited, and provided encouragement—thank you.

I take all the responsibility for any errors I have introduced along the way.

Foreword

As early as the seventeenth century, a British Quaker named Margaret Fell argued in an essay—"Women's Speaking Justified"—that the Bible has been misinterpreted with regard to women. By the 1970s there was a well-developed critique of traditional gender limitations on women, spearheaded by groups such as The Evangelical Women's Caucus and then later by Christians for Biblical Equality. While these Christians remained conservative in their theology, they argued that, properly understood, the Bible supports mutual submission in marriage and that there are many examples of women leaders in the early church—even in the writings of Paul.

That movement created a generation of conservative Christian women who expected equality in marriage and in the church. Even people who reject "biblical feminism" are influenced by this movement as more thought and attention is given to the role of women in the church.

My own research has focused on women who, having grown up expecting equality, sought to serve the church as ministers and teachers, only to find that their positions created controversy, tension, and turmoil. Many of the women I interviewed were transformed when they first read interpretations of biblical texts that argued for equality between men and women. They reported a sense of tremendous freedom when they came to see Jesus as the "first feminist."

While many conservative Christian women embrace female submission and separate roles for men and women, many others find those teachings violate their sense of self and even their sense of calling. They find it hard to reconcile the limitations with the view that women really are as important to God as men.

The argument that there are various ways to interpret the biblical passages pertaining to women has often been framed in ways designed for leaders. Christian women in the pews face the same issues as female leaders, albeit in different forms. While many of the books on this topic are not written for them, *Saving Women from the Church* is.

Susan McLeod-Harrison challenges contemporary conservative Protestant views about women, their proper roles, and their relationship to men and to churches. The author is herself a conservative Christian and *Saving Women from the Church* developed over the years out of her own experience. She challenges contemporary church practices (and the actions of contemporary fellow Christians) that would discount the value of women and their contributions. She does so through the application of principles she draws from the Bible.

Conflict over the roles of women has become an internal "culture war" within American conservative Protestantism. *Saving Women from the Church* is for women in the pews who feel caught in the crossfire.

> Julie Ingersoll
> associate professor of religious studies
> University of North Florida
> author of *Evangelical Christian Women:
> War Stories in the Gender Battles*

Introduction

I began writing this book in my mid-twenties, as a single Christian woman trying to identify her place in the church. I often felt alienated as I sat in a pew, looking up at the always-male pastors and preachers. I heard—in several churches and denominations—messages like these directed to women: "Wives, you are to submit to your husbands"; or "Women and men have different roles due to the creation order, but that doesn't mean they aren't *spiritual* equals"; or "The husband is the head of the home and this means he is to be the 'tie-breaker' for decision making." One time at a camp meeting, an elder's wife ventured a response to the usual "women are the 'helpmeet' of men" (from Genesis 2:18). She said, "I heard that *helper* in that Genesis passage is the same Hebrew word used to describe God as our help." The pastor ignored her accurate comment, in effect invalidating her words.

These erroneous and damaging messages hurt and confused me, and evoked difficult questions:

- What does it mean to be a woman in the church?
- Does God value men more than women?
- Does God love me as much as God loves my male pastor, my male elders, and my male friends?

The pain I felt from these unanswered questions caused me to consider leaving the church and even Christianity. I felt bound, however, because I did not doubt Christ's reality. To find a solution, I spent much time reading books by egalitarian Christians, as well as books by those who had conservative views on women. But both sides seemed biased. Which view was based on accurate scholarship? That question haunted me; I didn't yet have the biblical training to answer it, but my emotional pain was sharp and isolating.

I experienced a turning point when I reread the book of Luke and discovered that Jesus interacted positively with many different kinds of women. I knew there was something here for me to meditate on, even though I didn't yet understand all the implications.

Around the same time, I decided to do something about my sense of alienation at church. I spoke with my pastor about my discomfort with some of the things he said about women from the pulpit, and, despite my inner uncertainties about God's view of women, I asked if I could teach a Sunday school class on the issue of women and the Bible. The pastor told me, "Sure, go ahead. But no one will agree with you." Given the doubtful nature of his approval for the class, I decided to avoid contentious passages from Paul and go to the source—Christ himself. Who can disagree with Christ? So a group of about twelve women, my coteacher, and I spent ten weeks looking at how Jesus interacted with women.

During these weeks, my relationship with God started to heal as I began to realize that Jesus affirmed the full humanity and dignity of women. As I meditated on the truth that Jesus is "the exact representation" of God (Hebrews 1:3; see also 2 Corinthians 4:4; Colossians 1:15), I began to experience, through Jesus, God's deep love for me as a human and as a woman. As a lifelong Christian, I believed that Jesus is God, yet, emotionally, I had turned God and Jesus into two very different beings. For me, Jesus was the approachable, Human One I could trust, and God was the distant Father who had already judged me. But Jesus shows us that God is the warm, loving, forgiving Friend we have always wanted—one who tells us the truth but never without understanding and accepting us at the deepest level. Jesus said, "Anyone who has seen me has seen the Father" (John 14:9; see also John 1:1, 5:19, 12:45). Believing that truth on a deeper level helped me to trust God. The Jesus of the Gospels clearly loved and respected women as much as he did men, even though the same may not be true of Christians today.

Teaching the class did not help me feel less alone, however, even though it was clear that the women who attended had a deep thirst to know God loved them as women. When I found the organization Christians for Biblical Equality (CBE), I realized I wasn't alone in my perceptions that women were being treated as inferior people in the church. Many women feel alienated at church when they are not loved with the love that Jesus showed women. Some of the bias against women is due to ignorance and some to sin—a very old sin.

Through the centuries, Christians have placed greater emphasis on men being made in God's image than they have on women being made in God's image. Though the early church elevated the status of women,[1] as time went on church leaders began to minimize and even deny that women, too, are made in God's image. For example:

- St. Augustine said that a woman, without her husband, does not reflect the image of God.[2]

- Thomas Aquinas wrote that women were not fully made in God's image, because "man is the beginning and end of woman; as God is the beginning and end of every creature."[3]

- Even in this last century, Lutheran theologian Emil Brunner said, "It is certain that the Creator who has created body and soul as a unity, has also created the mental and spiritual nature of woman different from that of man."[4]

For humans to be made in God's image implies great intrinsic worth. It also implies uniqueness: Humans are different from animals. Humans are made for loving

---

[1] For example, Priscilla is a teacher (of "a learned man, with a thorough knowledge of the Scriptures") as recorded in Acts 18:24; Junia is an apostle whom Paul respects (Paul's "fellow Jew," "outstanding among the apostles," and "in Christ before I was," according to Romans 16:7); and Phoebe is a minister (διακονοσ) at the church in Cenchreae ("She has been a benefactor of many people, including me," says Paul in Romans 16:2).

[2] *The Trinity*, 12:10.

[3] *The Summa Theologica*, 1a, 93:4.

[4] Emil Brunner, *The Divine Imperative* (Philadelphia: Westminster Press, 1947) 375.

relationships with God and each other, as well as to be cocreators with God on earth. They are potentially a reflection of God's qualities of goodness, self-reflective intelligence, and creativity. Denying the full image of God in another person is ultimately to see that person as less than human.

The message that many church fathers and theologians passed down to the church today, however, is that women are not made in God's image in the way that men are. The implication is that women are less than human—inferior to men (the standard for a normal human being) in intelligence, personality traits, and in body. These inequalities require the submission of wives to husbands and to male spiritual leaders. The contemporary language of "spiritual equality, but different roles" does not change the underlying message of inferiority, as the roles differ fundamentally in who has power (such as decision-making power and economic power) in the relationship.[5]

It is sad and painful to say, but church traditions about women's inferiority to men may have been accepted most fully by Christian women themselves. Sarah

---

[5] The power to care for children is often given to women, but these children then miss out on being parented by their fathers and suffer emotional consequences. Mothers, too, find themselves missing out on the fullness of life that comes with balance. Everyone needs adult interaction and creativity. Additionally, these children see their mothers in a relatively powerless role compared with their fathers, and so in the end lose respect for their mothers despite the fact that mothers in these situations are usually the primary disciplinarians. For a different model of parenting that is now taking hold in the wider culture, see the book *Father Courage: What Happens When Men Put Family First* (New York: Harcourt, 2000) by Suzanne Braun Levine.

Sumner, a Christian scholar and minister, writes of her journey of discovering her own prejudice against women.[6] One of her first wake-up calls was at an anti-feminist women's conference, when she asked a group of women at her lunch table if women were inferior to men. To her shock, most of them said yes. She related this same story to a nationally prominent ministry leader, and this powerful woman then had an "aha" moment in which she realized that she, too, had "held back" because of viewing herself as inferior to men. My husband, who teaches undergraduates in the religion department of an evangelical university, has noted how often it is young women themselves who argue with him most vigorously against their own equality with men.

Why? One reason is that females hear this message repeatedly from girlhood onward. Just knowing that boys think being called a "girl" is the worst of insults plays lots of tricks on a female child's self-image. Other reasons have to do with church traditions, which include culture-based interpretations and translations of Scripture.

One culture-based reason for the belief that women are inferior to men is the frequent inaccurate translation of Genesis 1:27, which is well-translated as: "So God created human beings in his own image, in the image of God he created them; male and female he

---

[6] Sarah Sumner, *Men and Women in the Church* (Chicago, IL: InterVarsity Press, 2003), 72-73. Note that I do not agree with some of Sumner's biblical conclusions, but her honesty about her own journey toward realizing her prejudice against women is exemplary.

created them." Many Bible translations, however, use the words *man* and *him* instead of *human beings* and *them* in this verse. *Man* and *him* in today's English do not reflect the inclusive nature of the Hebrew in this verse.[7] Misreadings of 1 Corinthians 11 have also contributed to the historical argument that women are not fully made in God's image.

It is important to note as well that believers and non-believers alike have assumed that because Jesus was male in his humanity, and because we use masculine metaphors and pronouns for God, that God is gendered as a male, or at least predominantly masculine. But "God is spirit" (John 4:24), and is no more a literal male than Jesus is a literal son. (In other words, God does not have male sex organs.) "Father" language does not capture the totality of God any more than the metaphor of "Shepherd" captures all of who Jesus is. The fact that women are made in God's image means that feminine metaphors for God equally reflect the nature of God.[8]

The church has been slow to see these things. In the twentieth century, it was the secular feminist movement that tried to change the pervasive cultural belief that women are inferior to men and not as deserving of human rights (such as being able to vote, and work in

---

[7] There are primarily two translations of the Bible which use inclusive language (unless the original text specifies otherwise): the New Revised Standard Version (NRSV) and Today's New International Version (TNIV). I highly recommend purchasing one of these very accurate translations, as language has a powerful effect on self-image.

[8] I highly recommend the book *Is It Okay to Call God "Mother"? Considering the Feminine Face of God* (Peabody, MA: Hendrickson Publishers, 1993) by Paul Smith for further clarification on this important issue.

any way in which they are gifted). Yet, for a variety of reasons, evangelical women and men have sometimes vehemently shunned the term *feminist*.[9]

Regardless of our view of the various strands of the feminist movement, feminism has positively affected women in much of the industrialized world. We are more self-confident because of some of the victories of the feminist movements throughout the nineteenth and twentieth centuries: we can vote, we can participate in sports, we can earn university degrees, we can succeed in chosen occupations, and if we choose family life, we can coparent and comanage households with our husbands.

Because of this change in the way we see ourselves, some Christians rarely think about Paul's seemingly exclusionary commands regarding women. They write off these verses as cultural aberrations. Others are troubled by the implications of those verses for who God created women to be, or who God is. They ask themselves, *Why is it, again, that women can't lead or teach in the church?* And even, *Would a God who loves women really say such a thing?* Still others resist all but the most traditional interpretations of the passages, yet are privately aware of the tension of naming some Pauline commands to women as cultural (wearing "coverings" in

---

[9] Often, the term *feminist* conjures up images of women who are pro-abortion, uncommitted to their children, and/or are homosexual. The feminist movement, however, is more complex than those stereotypes. The more recent emphasis on "abortion rights" is a part of the movement that is ironically nonfeminist in that abortion has become a "quick-fix" in a society that does not properly value either women or children. But there are pro-life feminists who have a broader vision: pro-woman and pro-child.

church—1 Corinthians 11:2-16), others as universal (no woman leading or teaching a man in church—1 Timothy 2:8-15), and still others as vague and difficult to interpret (does "headship" really mean the husband is the "tie-breaker"?—1 Corinthians 11:3; Ephesians 5:21-33). Each of these groups can espouse their own views of why Paul said that "women will be saved through childbearing—if they continue in faith, love, and holiness with propriety" (1 Timothy 2:15) and disagree with each other passionately.

Despite the intellectual disagreements, many of us share the same questions in our deepest heart: Am I respected and loved by God and Christians the way I would be if I were male? Can I be myself with God? Can I be myself in the church? Is it okay to be strong and use my leadership gifts? Can I take a chance in the church, and fail without it being attributed to my gender?

It was years before I found a church where I could say yes to all those questions on an experiential level. But, long prior to that, I gained a deeper certainty about the answers to these questions in the same Bible that had caused me so much confusion about my own worth. And that's when I began writing this book.

For me, the key to understanding Scripture was learning about the biases of the culture in which Jesus grew up. I could then see his countercultural view of women more clearly. It is difficult to say exactly what life was like for Jewish women in Greco-Roman Palestine, because we don't know the stories of these women in their own voices. The laws of the Roman Empire and the religious laws and writings of Judaism, however, both indicate that generally women were given a much lower social status than men. Legally, women were their husband's property. They had few rights at all, and this was generally attributed to their inferiority. In Greco-Roman culture, respectable women were not to be seen in public. The virtuous woman submitted to her husband, cooked, cleaned, and cared for children in the home. These isolating social norms impacted Jewish women. In addition, despite the diversity of rabbinic opinions, the Jewish worldview was hierarchical, with women always under men in status. Rabbis had much to say about women's roles because they were seen as the means to control male sexual immorality. If a man sinned sexually, a woman was to blame. Jewish women usually could not initiate divorce, though one Jewish school of thought said a man could divorce his wife for cooking a dinner he disliked! Spiritually, women were seen as unequal to men. An old rabbinic prayer included giving thanks that the rabbi was not born a woman, because women (like slaves) were not thought worthy to study the Torah.[10]

---

[10] I want to emphasize that Judaism is not any more culturally biased against women than any other religion. Also, Judaism prioritized morality over rituals such as those surrounding purity laws (see Hyam Maccoby, *Ritual and Morality: The Ritual Purity System and Its Place in Judaism* [Cambridge, U.K.: Cambridge University Press, 1999]). Hence, Jesus' law of love was profoundly Jewish, even though it was sometimes disregarded in Judaism as it is sometimes disregarded in Christianity.

Jesus rejected such cultural norms without apology. In Matthew 15:2-3, the Pharisees and scribes challenged Jesus: "Why do your disciples break the tradition of the elders? They don't wash their hands before they eat!" Jesus replied, "And why do you break the command of God for the sake of your tradition?" Jesus freely overstepped cultural and religious expectations if those expectations kept him from fulfilling the law of love in his relationships with everyone, including women (see Matthew 22:34-40).

I wrote this book to help you see what I saw: Jesus followed the law of love and shunned cultural or religious expectations when they denigrated or limited women—and Jesus' love is the same today. Each chapter opens with two stories. The first illustrates a dilemma that women in the church can face when hurtful church traditions, age-old human biases, and profound misreadings of Scripture define how women should be treated.[11] The second, a fictionalized version of a biblical story, illustrates how Jesus treated a woman suffering a somewhat parallel injustice. As you read the stories, try to identify the difference between a cultural value (often "law"-oriented) and God's value (always love-oriented).[12]

---

[11] These stories all have kernels of real women's experiences in them, but the characters are fictional, and not based on actual women.

[12] If you feel uneasy about this differentiation between law and love, read these passages, which highlight how love fulfills the law: Matthew 7:12; Matthew 22:36-40; Mark 12:28-34; Romans 13:8-10; Galatians 5:14; Galatians 6:2.

After the two stories, you will find the following sections designed to deepen your understanding:

Just what was Jesus doing?—This section helps connect the ancient and contemporary stories, and points out the ways in which Jesus followed the law of love in his interactions with women. It gives cultural background information that will help you more fully understand Jesus' countercultural view.[13]

Questions for Reflection/Discussion—These are meant to help you think more deeply about the story and the biblical text and apply what you learn to your life and relationship with God.

Meditation for Healing—These are opportunities to invite Jesus to bring healing from the wounds you may have received in the church or in another Christian setting.

I pray that as you read these stories and reflect, you will feel God's tender love for and delight in women, who are created in God's own image.

---

[13] While this information comes from a variety of sources, a good deal of credit should go to Craig S. Keener's *The IVP Bible Background Commentary: New Testament* (Downers Grove, IL: InterVarsity Press, 1994), as I often found myself returning to it as a reliable reference. Another very helpful resource was Tal Ilan's *Jewish Women in Greco-Roman Palestine* (Peabody, MA: Hendrickson Publishers, 1996).

If you've felt alienated and judged in church...

chapter 1

Should I sit some place new today? The thought made me shiver slightly, and I pulled my arms in close to my body and decided against it. I headed toward the left side, back row, near the aisle, sat down, and turned off my cell phone. My teenage children, who had sworn off church, often called for any reason at all, such as not being able to find the ketchup in the fridge.

When the low hum of chatter faded into silence, a man seemed to be speaking from far away and saying, "Mwah mwah mwah mwah mwah," like the teachers in the *Peanuts* TV cartoons. The chords of "Amazing Grace" wooed me into semi-alertness and I sang automatically.

After the song was over, the emcee said, "Welcome visitors! We want you to feel at home here, and we hope you'll enjoy the service as much as we enjoy having you here." He had said the same thing every Sunday for the past two months. And then, like always, there was the excruciating "visiting" time when everyone shook hands or hugged. A couple of times people had welcomed me with a cheery, "Good morning!" but I normally managed to avoid this by returning to a meditative posture with the bulletin.

Today was different. A woman whose perfume announced her presence came and sat down beside me. She lifted my limp left hand, squeezed it, and said, "I've seen you across the church for several weeks now and wanted to come and invite you to our Women's Auxiliary meetings. And your husband could come to the weekly men's breakfasts we have. I'd be glad to introduce him to Artie."

I felt like someone had dropped by my house unexpectedly when I had no makeup on. I looked up and straight ahead at the large, plain, brown cross on the baptistry. Out of the corner of my eye, the woman seemed like a perfectly-coiffed Macy's mannequin, willing to wait an eternity. She continued to hold my sweaty left hand. When would she realize that there was no wedding band there?

"Um. My husband and I…are…divorced," I finally sputtered. "I know God hates divorce!" I had heard it over and over from friends, neighbors, relatives, and above all, my pastor. It was better to say it myself before anyone else could. "But my husband was terribly abusive," I finished softly. It was none of her business, but somehow I felt I had to tell her this to even have a chance of being accepted in this church.

"Oh, honey, it couldn't have been bad enough to divorce!" she said. "Why, Artie is no saint to live with either, but we've been married thirty years. It's just better for everyone if you stay together. That's the woman's job, you know," she continued, and patted my knee. "We keep the family together. We're peacemakers. I'm sure it's not too late for you and your husband too," she said.

By then, the strains of "Blessed Assurance" were beckoning the crowd to return to their seats. I couldn't think of a reply. I didn't have to, because when I looked up again, the woman was gone.

My face flushed into what must have been a deep pink. I felt so ashamed. I, an elder's wife for fifteen years, divorced! Sarah Hancock, devoted wife and mother, organ-player, bulletin-writer, cookie-maker, Sunday school teacher—divorced. Why did I even bother trying to be a part of the church anymore? Why did I keep coming back? *They don't want me here! I'm not welcome!* I thought.

A train of memories and thoughts captivated my attention the rest of the service. I pictured my ex-husband, in a parallel, but very different world. He remained an elder, immovable as a steeple, at my former church. I saw him now belting out some song, maybe "How Great Thou Art." His voice always overpowered everyone else's in the row. And then as he was singing I saw his expression change to rage, as though he could see me now. He began to hit me with his ringed fist, everywhere that was covered by clothing. This was the way Sundays had often ended in our home.

"Why did you wear that sultry silk blouse to church today, Sarah?" This is how it would start. Or "What's with the red lipstick?" "What do you think people are going to say about me at church, if you keep making mistakes like that on the organ?" "I noticed a typo in the bulletin. What's wrong with you? Are you trying to make me look like I married a fool?"

If I said nothing, he would go on and on, his voice rising louder and louder. If I defended myself, he would pick another thing to criticize. Either way, I would eventually get hit. The kids would retreat to their rooms or leave the house, or sometimes try to come to my defense. These were the worst days, when they would get involved.

The day before we all left him, my fourteen-year-old son must have heard me yelling out. He came flying out of his room like he was on fire and put my husband in a chokehold. Our son is thin and only five feet five inches, so my husband plied his arms off fairly easily before he threw him against the wall, holding our son by the collar, threatening to kill both my boy and me.

What would I have done without the women in my domestic violence support group? Most of them aren't even believers. But they have been a shelter in my emotional tsunami. Just last week I told them about what had happened when I called my quilting buddy at church to ask her if we could get together. I just wanted to explain to her why I had divorced my husband; I knew she'd heard rumors that weren't true. My "friend" refused and hung up the phone. I knew that if Lucy could reject me, anyone would.

After I told my support group about this, one woman, a pediatric cardiologist (she left her husband because all the head injuries he had given her started affecting her memory), said, "You need to get rid of the church entirely, Sarah. Has anyone there even asked your side of the story, or seen you at all for who you really are, rather than just the wicked woman who divorced her righteous husband?" The curls of her hair bobbed back and forth as she spoke. She was angry—with me, it seemed.

Suddenly I felt as on-the-spot as I had in my pastor's office, sitting in that luxurious black leather chair and being told to "submit" to my husband's violent ways.

"Well, probably not," I answered. "But I love the church. I love God. This is who I am," I said, and then I ventured, "Are you sure *you* appreciate who I really am?"

I was thankful when the group leader said, "Sarah does love the church, despite all the hurt she's experienced there. It's up to her if she wants to keep trying to be a part of it."

But now, as I sat with tears in my eyes, surrounded by strangers and the drone of a sermon I could not really hear, I wondered for the first time if the cardiologist was right.

» *feeling alienated and judged* «

One Sabbath a crippled woman stood among the crowd gathered outside the synagogue, clasping her hands together as if shaking hands with herself. She had walked bent over for a long time.

As she waited, enfolded into herself like a flower ready for spring, she heard the familiar whispering.

"There's the woman with an evil spirit."

"My mother said it runs in her family," another voice said.

The woman hobbled along to get away from the gossipers, her eyes cast down. She considered the dirt and grass, the colorful flowers and passing insects, to be God's gifts to her. Even now she gazed down at her dirty feet as if they were old friends.

She had not come to synagogue today to hear Jesus, but because she came every Sabbath. Sometimes she would hear a word from Scripture that she could recite throughout her week, gleaning great comfort. She particularly liked the latter part of Isaiah. Just the week before she had memorized this: "The Lord will surely comfort Zion and will look with compassion on all her ruins; he will make her deserts like Eden, her wastelands like the garden of the Lord."[1]

She entered the synagogue and found her place in the women's loft. Something about Jesus' voice made

---

[1] Isaiah 51:3.

her want to look at him. He was telling a story about a farmer who sowed seeds in the ground, and what happened to the different seeds. In the middle of his story, he became silent. She heard the women around her changing positions, as though they were looking around at one another in questioning ways. Unable to contain her curiosity, she positioned her body so she could raise her head and see the teacher down below.

Jesus caught her eye, an action as unexpected and impossible as any miracle, and then he said, "Woman, please come here." She saw the surprised faces of the men, below, turn to look up at her. She closed her eyes, longing to simply disappear. One woman whispered, "It's you the teacher is calling!" She took an unwilling step and then hobbled through the gazing, whispering women, down the stairs, and up to the front, her eyes still on her feet. Her thoughts whirled. What had she done? What would this teacher say to her; how might he humiliate her?

She anguished at the stares of so many men and women. Collective whispers sent waves of shame over her. As she came within a few steps of Jesus, he spoke to her: "Woman, you are set free from your infirmity."

She jerked away as she felt warm hands on her spine—such an odd sensation. She knew only the touch of squirrels as they ventured near and perched on her back to be fed breadcrumbs. She had never come this near to a rabbi. What would people say about her now? Then she felt a mighty gale, the power of magicians and the prophets, move in her. As it flashed through her, something else—a thing that had been choking the life out of her—rushed out. She heard her body healing before she could discern what was happening; her back cracked several times and settled her into perfect posture. The inward space where she slept, ate, breathed, and dialogued with herself and her gray emotions began to fill up with light and love. Inexplicably, she felt as though she had been perfectly loved these past eighteen years, as though she had never been alone.

Turning around and gazing without fear into Jesus' attentive, dark eyes, she spoke words that sprouted up from her deepest heart, "Praise the God of Israel! God is my help and my deliverer!" She looked at the open-mouthed, amazed faces of the men who were now standing, and the women above who were pressed around each other. She could see it in their expressions—she who had been shameful was now unsurpassingly honorable. God had chosen *her*. Her smile erupted into laughter, igniting a dozen more flames of joyful laughter around the room.

But not everyone was happy about the miracle that had just unfolded. The synagogue ruler stood at the back of the room, arms crossed, eyebrows furrowed. He was fine with healings. But he was there to keep order, to make sure the people obeyed the law. Did not this fellow know what time of the week it was? Besides, why had Jesus healed a woman, an old, barren spinster at that?

The ruler himself suffered from pain in his feet. Wasn't he far worthier of healing?

He walked up in front of Jesus, partly blocking him from view. He was taller than Jesus, but the ruler's presence was diminished in light of Jesus' power and the woman's joy. Nonetheless, with a crooked finger in the air, and his other hand clutching the scrolled Torah, he lifted his head and shouted, "There are six days for work. So come and be healed on those days and not on the Sabbath."

With one long stride Jesus was at the ruler's side, fixing an angry gaze upon him and then upon certain others in the crowd. "You hypocrites! Doesn't each of you on the Sabbath untie your ox or donkey from the stall and lead it out to give it water? Then should not this woman—" Jesus gestured toward her, "a daughter of Abraham, whom Satan has kept bound for eighteen long years, be set free on the Sabbath day from what bound her?"

The ruler and those who were against Jesus cast their eyes downward, as if the afternoon light from the windows was too bright. The common people reflected another light, looking again and again to see the shining face of the healed woman.[2]

---

[2] A fictionalized version of Luke 13:10-17.

Just what was Jesus doing?

The religious people around both Sarah and the "bent-over" woman pronounced judgments against these women—even in the women's suffering—that left the women feeling alienated from community. The bent-over woman had likely heard, for "eighteen long years," that she was shameful due to a physical condition caused by an evil spirit—a condition completely beyond her control. Sarah also had an unshakeable shame over her new status as "divorced," and was quick to quote Malachi 2:16 which she had heard again and again. (Her shame was likely compounded by the abuse, as women often blame themselves for it).

Sarah had not heard the latter part of that declaration: "'I hate divorce,' says the Lord God of Israel, 'and I hate it when people clothe themselves with injustice,' says the Lord Almighty." The conviction that Jesus condemned divorce often comes from a lack of knowledge about the injustices prevalent in Jesus' time. When Jesus said, "Therefore what God has joined together, let no one separate" (Mark 10:9), it is likely he wanted to protect women and children from poverty. In Jesus' day women were usually economically dependent on their husbands. Jewish law allowed a man to divorce his wife for any reason ("It was because your hearts were hard that Moses wrote you this law," Mark 10:5). Women normally could not initiate divorce themselves (although they could sometimes do so with the help of a male family member), so divorce really was about the "hardness of heart" of husbands and fathers (see Matthew 5:31-32). That's likely why the twelve disciples seemed uncomfortable when Jesus spoke against divorce (Matthew 19:10; Mark 10:1-12).

While this doesn't make arbitrary divorce "okay," it does imply that Jesus was very concerned with justice issues for women. He was willing to "break the law" (the law that men could divorce their wives for any reason) in order to bring about justice for women. In light of this, it's reasonable to assume that a person is not breaking Jesus' law of love in obtaining a divorce in order to escape an abusive marriage.

Divorce is certainly not the only reason hurting women feel at odds when they are in church or around a group of Christians. I focus on divorce, however, because it is such a common occurrence, and yet despite this reality divorced people in the church still carry a "mark," even when they did not initiate the divorce or were divorced through no fault of their own.

There are many other reasons women might feel judged and alienated in church. Some feel like outcasts because they have a history of being abused sexually, even by a respected church member or leader. Sometimes girls and women are not believed or are told to "just forgive" their abuser (even if he continues to abuse freely), and so the victims either "stuff" their anger and hurt, or they feel forced out of the church. Some church leaders prefer to forsake a hurt girl or woman rather than confront an abusing but powerful church member.

The Gospels show us that Jesus had a different perspective. He became particularly angry when religious leaders misused their power and religious followers who had little power suffered for it (see Luke 17:1-3). But he did more than just get angry. He loved.

In order to show God's love, as well as the difference between tradition and love, Jesus "broke the rules" for the bent-over, outcast woman who bore not only her illness but the judgments of others. She likely had no real place in her society, perhaps being unable to do the things that gave a woman a minimal amount of respect (such as cooking and cleaning). It is quite possible she was—as I suggest in the narrative—without husband or children. Hence, when Jesus saw her, he felt her suffering as well, on every level. He loved her with a love that fulfilled every law, even as he broke cultural and religious laws right and left.

It was frowned upon for a rabbi to touch, or even talk to, a woman who was not his wife, yet Jesus touched this woman to heal her. When he called the unnamed woman "a daughter of Abraham" (Luke 13:16), he broke the "gender rules" as "son of Abraham" was a term reserved for male Jews. (Every woman present must have held her head a little higher that day!) Jesus also shamed those among his opponents who were particularly concerned with their status (Luke 13:17). Most significantly, in order to love this woman Jesus appeared to break the Sabbath (Luke 13:14) and garnered public rebuke for doing so. When he stopped in the middle of his sermon because he noticed the woman and her pain, Jesus' loving compassion taught those in attendance more than any sermon about true religion could (see James 1:27).

Jesus message was and is: *Love supersedes every cultural law.* Like Sarah's husband, like her pastor and her quilting friend Lucy, the synagogue ruler and others claimed to love God and to be obedient, but they refused to love their fellow human beings (see 1 John 2:9; 4:20). They valued law over love (see Matthew 22:37-40). Jesus, however, embraced the wounded outcast. He, too, experienced rejection in the very places he should have been welcomed (Mark 6:1-6; Luke 4:16-30).

Questions for Reflection/Discussion

1. What "cultural laws" did Jesus break in order to love the bent-over woman?

2. What "cultural laws" in our churches make it likely that hurting women (and men) will feel alienated from and unloved by others?

3. What similarities do you see between the divorced woman and the bent-over woman? Of the two, whom do you relate to more, and why?

4. Have there been times in your life when you have felt judged and alienated in the church because of your gender, marital status, ethnicity, life circumstances, sins, hurts, addictions, appearance, or physical disability? What made you (or makes you) feel this way? In light of what you have just read, what do you think Jesus thinks and feels about how you may have been (or are being) treated?

5. How are Sarah's husband, the pastor, and Lucy similar to the religious leaders and the synagogue ruler? Have you ever acted in a way similar to them? How so?

Meditation for Healing

Find a place where you can relax. Invite the Holy Spirit to come close and to help you be aware of being in Jesus' presence. (Even if you don't *feel* Jesus' presence, go ahead and affirm that presence.) Use whatever medium (writing, drawing, picturing in your mind, singing) works for you to envision the following scene: Jesus is preaching a sermon in your church, or any church. In the middle of a sentence, he sees you in the crowd, your eyes meet, and he stops speaking. He calls your name and asks you to come forward. In front of everyone, he calls you by a name meaningful to you and others (Favored Daughter, Compassionate One, Courageous Daughter of God, and so on). Then he heals you of whatever is hurting you—physically or emotionally. Everyone present can see that he loves you and has given you "a spirit of power, love, and self-discipline" (2 Timothy 1:7). Someone who represents those who have discriminated against you or rejected you stands up and objects to Jesus empowering you, a woman, and Jesus points out very explicitly the hypocrisy shown by this objection. Everyone else (not only the women, but the men as well!) is on your side and delighting in what Jesus did for you.

If you've believed women are inferior to men...

chapter 2

Sunday's church service had been rough. During the final worship song, I had felt so disheartened that I'd lost the wonderful "loved" feeling I'd had ever since I met Jesus six months earlier. After we'd been dismissed, I pulled my navy blue beret over my curls and walked straight out the back door. I felt distinctly *un*loved. I was thankful I had Rebecca to turn to now. I'd met her the night I had first thought about becoming a Christian, after her campus Christian group put on a talk called "Satisfying Sex."

She and I were meeting every Monday at the Blue Angel Café—right around the corner from the university we attended—for lunch and "discipling." Before I met Christ and started studying the Bible with Rebecca, I had been planning to teach high school history. But I so enjoyed Bible study that I had decided to major in classical languages and eventually become a New Testament professor in a Bible college. I spent so much time reading the Bible, I was getting a *C* in my history class.

These Monday lunches were high points for me. I always enjoyed the leafy, crunchy walk from my class to the café. I breathed in the sharply cool autumn air, and filled my lungs with hope. Soon I was walking through the saloon-type doors and looking around the dark room for Rebecca.

"Hey, Julie! Over here!" Rebecca said.

I walked over to her and she gave me a hug, like usual. We weren't huggers in my family, but I liked how Christians are always hugging each other.

"I *really* need to talk to you today!" I told her as we took our seats.

"So what's up? What are you thinking about this week?"

I leaned forward, glancing sideways as though someone might overhear me, and said, "Yesterday my pastor gave this sermon on women, and he said something I don't understand. He said that women are *spiritually* equal to men, but have different roles. And he said one of our roles is to submit and to follow what the man says, or at least what the husband says. But what did he mean—'*spiritually* equal'? I've thought about it all yesterday and today and I don't get it."

Rebecca took out her black pocket Bible with the gilded pages, while saying, "I think he's just saying that we're all one in Christ Jesus. It's like that verse in Galatians, let me show you…" She turned the thin pages carefully. "Here it is: 'There is neither Jew nor Gentile, neither slave nor free, neither male nor female, for you are all one in Christ Jesus.'"[1]

I liked that verse a lot, but it seemed the pastor was saying the very opposite of it—that "male" and "female" mattered a whole lot. I said, "What I want to know is what is it we're *not* equal in, if we're only equal *spiritually*. Why is it that only women must submit to men and not the other way around as well, like in any other healthy relationship?"

"Well, men and women are just different, you know. We have different roles in life due to our different biology. We can have babies and men can't, and that alone makes us very different." She raised her eyebrows.

Her answer didn't satisfy me. After all, being different biologically isn't the same as being unequal in status. Men and women are both human. But rather than argue the point with her I asked, "But what does that have to do with submission?"

"I guess you're getting at the fact that some men think that women are inferior. But we know *that's* not true, right?" she laughed.

"Right, right, that's what I mean!" I said, emphasizing each word with my hands. I thought that maybe she was starting to understand me, but her next words squelched that hope.

"But we do have to submit, as women, and I think ultimately we just submit because that's what the Bible

---

[1] Galatians 3:28.

says we're supposed to do," Rebecca sighed as the words came out of her pink-lined, glossy mouth.

I took a deep breath, removed my glasses and cleaned the lenses carefully, thinking about all I had learned from Rebecca when I'd questioned her about weird commands in the Bible. After I put my glasses back on, I said, "But what about all that other stuff in the Bible that we don't actually do now? We don't give one another a holy kiss in church, right? And…a lot of people don't lift up their hands when they pray anymore—at least we don't in *my* church. Oh, and women don't wear head coverings in church and they speak in church all the time! What makes submission different, even though it also makes no sense?"

"Well, I guess those other things are cultural, but the command to submit to husbands is universal. We know that because women were created after men were; that's the creation order." Rebecca's voice took a perky sound with this last phrase, as though this should cheer me up.

I sighed. "What does being created *last* have to do with it? I thought God started with the most basic forms of creation and moved upward. And you said just last week that God was often choosing the second-born and the *least* likely to lead his people."

Rebecca laughed. "Well, yes, I did say that, and it's true." Looking down, she said, "But just not in this case."

Just as I realized our discussion couldn't go any further, the waiter brought us our meals. I respected my friend, but I knew something didn't ring true about what she was saying. I wasn't even sure *she* believed it. I certainly didn't believe that God had created men and women so differently that women always had to follow and men always had to lead. And a good marriage was supposed to be about partnership, anyway, not leading and following. I knew my own personality to be one of relying on information and logic for decision-making; all the women in my family are like this. And I knew from studying psychology that the stereotype about women being irrational or less intelligent than men isn't true.

Rebecca made small talk through most of the meal, but I was distracted by old thoughts that kept popping into my mind. "Christianity is for people in love with the 1950s," I used to say, snidely. Or another favorite, "You have to check your brain at the door of the church." I was amazed that Rebecca preferred a non sequitur to simple logic. Just obey everything in the Bible—even if it's absurd in our context? If women and men are equally likely to be intelligent and rational, there is no reason we should submit to men simply because we are women, whether in marriage or out.

By the time our meal was over, I was just as depressed as I had been on Sunday. It was dawning on me that a lot of Christians believed what my pastor and Rebecca did about a "woman's role." I wondered if there were any who *didn't*. I just wanted to leave and put us both out of our misery. I took the check and said, "It's my turn to pay!"

"Oh, yeah, okay. Thanks," Rebecca said in a subdued way. And then, "I know what we talked about today was hard, Julie. Especially for someone like you who is so smart. I'd been meaning, even, to talk to you about your plans to become a Bible professor. But that can wait until next week. See you then." And she walked out without looking back, the swinging doors falling into place behind her.

I stood there, unable to believe her words, as the check slipped out of my hand.

"Listen! He's gone from the tomb because he's alive again! I have seen the Lord!"

The men stared at Mary's swollen eyes and face, and then looked at one another for direction. Peter and John still had not returned to the others with a report on the empty grave, so the only "evidence" the other men had was the witness of a woman. Had Mary really seen Jesus, whom they had all seen cruelly crucified three days earlier? Or had her grief overwhelmed her and caused her to make this crazy assertion? After all, they reasoned, everyone knows that women are weak and easily overwhelmed—lightheaded, really.

Mary could see the disbelief and pity on the men's faces. For a few minutes she doubted herself and reviewed the events of the past hour. She remembered how Peter and John had run wildly to the tomb, but then had given up on finding Jesus. Only she had refused to leave. She stayed at the tomb while the men walked toward Peter's home, where they would comfort one another over a meal his wife was preparing.

Even though she remembered that Jesus said he would rise again after three days, she could not stop sobbing at the tomb. The evil cruelty of what had been done to Jesus made resurrection seem like wishful thinking. Determined that Jesus would at least have dignity in death, she stayed behind, shivering under a blanket just inside the entrance of the cave and almost chanting to herself, *Where, where, where is he? Where can they have taken his body?* Suddenly, from below, where Jesus' body had been placed, she saw a light emerge as though the sun was quickly rising. She wiped her tears away with her fingers and slowly made her way down the narrow staircase, asking, "Who's there?"

The light itself answered her, in the form of two angels. They were smiling as though they had expected her. Mary's heart pounded within her as she took in the sight, but disappointment filled her eyes with tears again. She had no interest in anything but looking for Jesus. She saw that the angels were sitting where his body had been, one at the head and one at the foot. Was Jesus now an angel? If so, why wasn't he with them? If not, what had they done with his body?

The angels interrupted her thoughts, asking, "Woman, why are you crying?"

"They have taken my Lord away, and I don't know where they have put him!"

Just then, Mary heard footsteps behind her and turned. The light of the angels was so bright that her eyes had to adjust in the relative darkness before she could see a very ordinary-looking man standing there.

"Woman, why are you crying?" he asked, just as the angels had. Mary wondered, *Do these men know nothing?* Was it really so strange that she should be grieving the horrific death of someone she loved?

The man tilted his head and looked straight into her eyes. "Who is it you are looking for?"

He must be the gardener, Mary thought. *Maybe he knows something, maybe he's seen someone, maybe he himself....* "Sir, if you have carried him away, tell me where you have put him, and I will get him!"

Just as he had spoken the first words before creation, the man spoke her name, "Mary."

The opaque barrier between them shattered, and she saw him for who he was. "Teacher!" She raised her arms and stepped forward to assure herself Jesus was not a ghost. She wanted to see the hands and wrists she'd seen so tortuously ripped open only days before.

But Jesus held up his scarred hands to stop her, saying, "Do not hold on to me, for I have not yet ascended to the Father. Go instead to my brothers, and tell them, 'I am ascending to my Father and your Father, to my God and your God.'"

Disappointment and hurt stilled her excitement. She simply wanted to touch him! Jesus was alive again...

but everything had changed. As Mary stood before the living Jesus with her arms outstretched, she finally began to truly understand who Jesus was—not only a man she loved deeply, but God's Son. The words Jesus had spoken again and again about his death and resurrection made sense for the first time.

Now she stared at the backs of the heads of the male disciples, smiling and chuckling to herself at her insider's knowledge. She knew Jesus had appeared to her, and that he was alive. Nothing in heaven or on earth could change that.[2]

---

[2] A fictionalized version of John 20:11-18, combined with aspects of Luke 24:1-12.

Just what was Jesus doing?

It has been said that culture is to humans what water is to fish—so pervasive as to be invisible. In Jesus' time, the notion of women's intellectual (as well as social, biological, and spiritual) inferiority to men was accepted as fact—it was part of the "water" everyone swam in. Few thought to question it. Josephus, a historian and Pharisee of the first century, had this to say about women: "The woman, says the Law, is in all things inferior to man. Let her accordingly be submissive."[3]

[3] *Apion*, 2.201.

Like the first-century Pharisee Josephus, Julie's pastor linked the idea of women's and men's inequality with the "woman's role" of being submissive to men. Josephus could be very direct, in his time, whereas now religious leaders say the same thing in gentler language ("spiritual equality but different roles"). One way Jesus rejects this oppressive and inaccurate interpretation of Scripture is through his treatment of Mary Magdalene. His acknowledgement of her as a disciple worthy to witness and proclaim the most important event in history tells the whole story: Women, made in God's image, do not have a subordinate role to men.

The Twelve, however, were men of their times. Luke's account of this story tells us that Mary Magdalene went to the tomb with two other women, Joanna and Mary the mother of James, and that the disciples didn't believe their report, discounting it as "nonsense" (Luke 24:11). It seems the men assumed the women were prone to idle tales. After all, due to a belief that women were imbecilic, women were not even allowed to be witnesses in a Roman court of law. Jewish law also exempted women's testimony about weightier matters due to women's "light-mindedness." So why should the men believe a woman when it came to something as important as this?[4]

---

[4] Both Peter and John, however, were spurred to go to the tomb upon reports from women (Luke 24:12; John 20:3-9). Peter was "amazed" (NRSV) and John "believed" based on the absence of the body in the tomb.

In light of these things, Christ's resurrected appearance to Mary, a woman in deep grief, was particularly meaningful. He must have known that the disciples were steeped in traditional beliefs about women's inferiority. Yet he chose to appear to a woman instead of to a man. Clearly, Jesus did not believe that Mary's gender or her expressive grief disqualified her as a rational witness of his resurrection.

The Bible doesn't state why Jesus chose to appear to a woman, or why he chose to appear to Mary in particular. The men had distanced themselves from Jesus at this point, however. They were afraid they would be the next "criminals" to be crucified due to their associations with Jesus (see John 20:19). The men had failed Jesus at the moment he needed them most. In contrast, Mary Magdalene (along with other women) watched him suffer and die (Mark 15:40-41; Matthew 27:55-56; John 19:25) and then Mary and other women disciples remained at the tomb. So Jesus appeared to one of his strongest and most faithful disciples at that time.

Cultural beliefs about women's inferiority could not stop Jesus Christ, who is God, from seeing and leaning on the inner strength and good mind of Mary Magdalene.

(For help interpreting the texts on submission in the epistles, see Appendix B).

Questions for Reflection/Discussion:

1. What "cultural laws" did Jesus break in order to make Mary Magdalene the first witness to his resurrection?

2. What "cultural laws" in our churches make it likely that women will feel inferior to men?

3. If you had a close friend whom you considered spiritually equal to you, but not intellectually or ontologically (in their very essence) fit to make decisions or initiate decisions having to do with her own life or your friendship, what would your friendship be like? How might this perspective affect your relationship if you were married to this person?

4. How do you feel toward the character Rebecca? What kinds of experiences might have led her to say, "I think ultimately we just submit because that's what the Bible says we're supposed to do?"

5. Do any of Julie's questions or concerns sound interesting to you? Which ones would you like to explore further?

Meditation for Healing

Find a place where you can relax. Invite the Holy Spirit to come close, until you are aware of being in Jesus' presence. (Even if you don't feel Jesus' presence, go ahead and affirm that presence.) Recall a time when you felt your intellectual, logical, or decision-making ability was called into question, simply because you are a woman. Or remember a time when you heard a hurtful sermon or statement from a church leader about female submission. You may have responded to these events with depression—like Julie did—or with anger, or both. Ask God to help you become aware of your feelings about these repeated insults in church.

Then picture yourself as Mary Magdalene, sharing your good news with the men. Imagine the male disciples are those who have hurt you in the past by discounting or ignoring your intelligence and capabilities. Perhaps one of the men is even your husband or father.

Imagine that Jesus himself shows up and vindicates you in that moment. He even reprimands the men for not seeing you as an equal, pointing out that after his resurrection he chose to appear to you first. He speaks affirming words to you ("You are made in my image,") and confirms that you are a faithful disciple and friend of Jesus. What is Jesus saying to you now? Ask Jesus to speak to your heart and bring healing.

If the church has resisted your call to minister...

chapter 3

"Should I go in, or should I go home?" I asked myself, tapping on the steering wheel with my French manicured fingernails. I always paid extra attention to my appearance because I knew from Pastor Joe that first impressions matter when you're talking with non-Christians. I had an appointment with him now. I admired my pastor like no one else. Even though we didn't talk very often, his sermons on evangelism had had a huge influence on me. I really wanted to be just like him. So this meeting weighed on me. I had something to tell him that was extremely near to my heart, but I sensed he would not approve of what I had to say.

I was watching the digital clock on the dashboard when I saw Gloria, Pastor Joe's secretary, carrying two coffee drinks in a cardboard container. She saw me and waved. I figured I'd better go in.

When I walked into his office, Pastor Joe looked up and closed his laptop with a click. "Erline! Come in!"

he said with his usual enthusiasm. He leaned back into his adjustable chair and took a long sip of his coffee—from the writing on the cardboard cup, it looked like a triple Americano.

Gloria walked in just then and picked up a huge pile of papers in the in-box. I like Gloria a lot. She wears five earrings on each ear and one in her eyebrow and has a tattoo (it says "Glory") on her right bicep. Despite her rebellious look, Gloria is an awesome secretary for Pastor Joe.

He himself looks less than traditional. He feels that sporting a long (albeit graying) ponytail and wearing jeans and a T-shirt every day make him more approachable to a variety of people, both in and out of the church. The real challenge and commitment of his life is to make Scripture relevant to people today and to win souls to Christ. I so resonate with that calling, though I prefer to dress up rather than dress down to make my "first impression."

"Sit down!" Pastor Joe said, beckoning warmly.

I sat on the edge of my seat and leaned forward. I crossed and uncrossed my legs, and then my arms. I hadn't been this nervous since the regional competition on the high school debate team.

"Well, just how *are* you, Erline? I haven't talked to you since your college graduation. What's new?" Pastor Joe said, smiling, as if in anticipation of good news.

"Pastor Joe," I said, smiling back. So far, so good. "The reason I want to talk with you is…well…I want your advice. I want to tell you about something I feel God calling me to do."

Pastor Joe nodded and said, "Oh, really? Forgive me if this sounds too forward, but are you dating someone now?"

I felt confused momentarily, but then said, "Well, no. Actually, it's more about life direction in general."

He waited silently for me to go on. After regaining my focus, I continued, "You know I've always had such a love for evangelism, right? Four people have come to Christ in just the last year at my college, did you know that?" I didn't want to say I had directly led them to Christ after giving a talk at school. I didn't want to brag. I hoped he would get my drift.

Pastor Joe said, "Really? I hadn't realized that. That's really cool."

While we were both on a positive note, I decided to just plunge in. "Pastor Joe, this is what I came to ask your advice about: I think God is calling me to be an evangelistic preacher!" Before then, I had not uttered these words to another soul, except God. I went on to tell Pastor Joe that I thought God might even want me to lead a city-wide revival, like a female Billy Graham. I said this was all I wanted to do for the rest of my life, offering these words to him like diamonds.

It turned out he thought they were just rocks.

Pastor Joe's smile disappeared and his eyes fixed unblinkingly upon me as he thought about what I had said. Finally his gaze shifted to the clear glass paperweight with the rose inside, sitting on his desk. With a furrowed brow, he said, "Erline, you have such a beautiful heart for the Lord. And you *are* a good speaker." Then he tilted his head as he asked, "But, really, don't you think there is much greater need overseas? Don't you think you might be more suited to be a missionary?"

I sighed. This was what I was afraid of. I couldn't think of any female role models at all—no one to point to and say, "Well, look at *her*! *She's* doing it!" Pastor Joe himself was my role model and distant mentor.

"Well," I ventured, "I don't really feel God calling me to leave this country. I know how crazy it must sound, but I just feel in my heart that this is what I was born to do." My voice volume had lowered, since I realized he was not going to share my excitement.

Pastor Joe tried again to win me over. "Erline, you know as well as I do, I'm sure, what the Bible says about a woman's role in life. It's not in leadership. As an evangelist you'd be leading men and teaching them the gospel." He finally broke that devastating stare of his—he used that stare from the pulpit when he had something to say that would hit hard.

"Look," he said, changing his demeanor, "When you get married—and I'm sure you will, you're a lovely, talented girl—you can help your husband in his ministry. Or you can develop a ministry to women. There's so much you can do, so much need." He went on to talk about all the needs at church right now—children's ministry, organizational ministry (organization wasn't *his* strength), visitors ministry, mercy ministry. When he saw the blank look on my face, he finally he revisited the idea of overseas missions work.

"If you joined a missions agency," he said, "I imagine you would be able to do a lot of things, maybe even preach. Who knows? Sometimes they have shortages of men to do what needs to be done."

The longer Pastor Joe went on in this hopeful, positive tone of voice, the more deflated I felt. I sank back into my chair as he talked. I prayed, "Jesus, help me say what I need to if this call is really of you."

In a moment, I found myself sitting back up and leaning forward again, as though there was a warm hand on my back pushing me forward just a bit. Pastor Joe was swiping at invisible crumbs on his desk.

"Pastor Joe, you're saying I can be an evangelist overseas. I can take leadership in explaining all the Scripture passages about Christ to both men and women, as long as it's in another culture. I could even preach and help these people grow up in Christ. But I'm just wondering, why is that sinful here? Was I even wrong to bring my male friends to faith in Christ?"

Joe chuckled and glanced up at the clock over the door, before looking back at me. "Oh, Erline. That's not what I said. I'm *so* glad you have a heart for the Lord; don't get me wrong. Really, God will use you and put you just where God wants you. You can do whatever you like for the Lord, as long as you're not leading or teaching men. Maybe you'll even meet some good-looking guy soon who God will call to be a traveling evangelist, and you can help him. God has everything under control. It will all work out!" He smiled warmly at me.

Pastor Joe's worn, leather Bible set on the desk between us. I thought, *Maybe he's right. Those verses are in there about women not being in leadership; why am I trying to fight the Word of God?* I felt as though Pastor Joe's friendly, kind words expressed a damning judgment that had been pronounced against me long ago.

My heart wilted as I rose from my chair, thanked Pastor Joe, and said goodbye.

As though she were well-prepared for such surprising meetings with strange men, Naomi walked casually with her head high.

I wonder if he's a good man. Her heart beat faster, but she slowed down. She lifted the stone that covered the well and set the stone on the well's edge, daring to glance sideways at the stranger. Relief washed over her when she saw that the man sitting on the ground near the well did not return her attention. She suspected from his facial structure that he was Hebrew. *He'll just ignore me.*

But then she jumped a bit when she heard the man's raspy, soft voice. "Will you give me a drink?" he asked. Naomi felt his eyes on her face as she lowered the smooth leather bucket into the cool water.

She heaved the bucket out of the well, set it down, and wiped her hands with a cloth. She glanced at his profile once more and said quietly, "You are a Jew and I am a Samaritan woman. How can you ask me for a drink?" She knew the Pharisees assumed Samaritan women to be "unclean." But seeing the man all slumped over on the ground, sweaty and dirty, she picked up the bucket again and handed it to him.

He cupped his hands and drank for a long time as Naomi watched and waited for an answer to her question. He wiped his mouth with his sleeve, then he looked up at her and said, "If you knew the gift of God and who it is that asks you for a drink, you would have asked him and he would have given you living water."

She squinted her eyes at him. Just who did this Jewish wisecracker think he was? Did he want to have some fun at her expense? She put her hands on her hips, like she had done since she was a little girl when she wanted to get a point across. "Sir," she said, pausing for effect, "You have nothing to draw with and the well is deep. Where can you get this living water? Are you greater than our father Jacob, who gave us the well and drank from it himself, as did also his sons and flocks and herds?"

The man held her bold gaze as though reading her life story through her eyes, and said, "Everyone who drinks this water will be thirsty again, but those who drink the water I give them will never thirst. Indeed, the water I give them will become in them a spring of water welling up to eternal life." He looked at her and waited.

She continued to stare point-blank at the man, just beginning to grasp the extraordinariness of this encounter. The intuition that she had followed in the past, despite the searing social consequences, filled her body like the water filled the well. She found herself saying words that did not make sense to her mind, yet did to her spirit: "Sir, give me this water so that I won't get thirsty and have to keep coming here to draw water."

"Go, call your husband and come back," he told her.

Almost before he was through speaking, she said, "I have no husband."

"You are right when you say you have no husband. The fact is, you have had five husbands, and the man you now have is not your husband. What you have just said is quite true." The man remained seated on the ground as he looked at her again carefully, waiting.

Naomi glared at him, tight-lipped, face reddening. Then her rage billowed into relief, when she remembered this man was a Jew and a stranger to her. *He could not know any of this. But then, God must know this. God knows about my life. But I don't want to talk about it to this man, no matter how holy he may be.*

Involuntary feelings washed over her. Her stomach muscles tensed as she recalled her five husbands, how she had trusted each one and each of them had divorced her. She was never able to be the quiet, humble, restrained kind of woman they assumed she'd be when they were first engaged. If her husband slept with a maidservant, she did not hold back angry words. If he hurt the children, she asked the compassionate religious leaders in the town to talk to him. If her mother-in-law made unreasonable demands, she argued with her. This last habit got her into the most trouble. Her husbands, of course, left her for less-difficult women.

Naomi turned away so the man could not see the tears in her eyes. She was intelligent and curious, and she defaulted to the intellectual when pressed. "Sir, I can see that you are a prophet. Our ancestors worshiped on this mountain," and she pointed to Mount Gerazim behind them, where the Jews had destroyed the Samaritan temple before her grandparents were born. "But you Jews claim that the place where we must worship is in Jerusalem." Though Naomi did not want to discuss her past, she knew this man could answer a question that had plagued her all her life. Without a temple, were they really worshiping God?

"Woman, believe me, a time is coming when you will worship the Father neither on this mountain nor in Jerusalem. You Samaritans worship what you do not know; we worship what we do know, for salvation is from the Jews. Yet a time is coming and has now come when the true worshipers will worship the Father in the Spirit and in truth, for they are the kind of worshipers the Father seeks. God is spirit and his worshipers must worship in the Spirit and in truth."

Naomi tried to put order to her thoughts as they raced to catch up with her feelings. It was as though this Jewish man was saying he knew that God was seeking her, a Samaritan woman, and that God knew she worshiped in the Spirit and in truth already. This man made her think of the Messiah, whom she had heard about from her mother since she was a baby. She said, more loudly than she had spoken before, "I know that Messiah is coming. When he comes, he will explain everything…to us…." Her last few words trailed off, as her spirit anticipated what he was about to say.

"I, the one speaking to you—I am he."

Despite the hot sun, Naomi felt chills, felt as though all the laws of nature had been reversed. Could the Messiah really be here in front of her, in the flesh? Why would he reveal himself to *her*?

Just then, Naomi noticed a group of men sauntering up to the well. Naomi could see them murmuring among themselves, disapproval written on their faces. A holy man talking to a Samaritan woman in private?

She wasn't about to let them spoil the amazing gift she had just been given, so she turned and ran back toward town. On her way Naomi stopped at farms, until she made her way to the town's center. To everyone she saw she said, "Come, see a man who told me everything I ever did. Could this be the Messiah?"

Men stopped working in the fields to talk to each other about Naomi's message. Women stopped grinding grain, baking, spinning, weaving, and cleaning. They called their children to stop playing and to come to them. In groups small and large, they hurried down the main road, toward the city gate, conversing excitedly with one another. Those near Naomi questioned her.

She could only describe the way this stranger knew about her life, and that he said he was the Messiah. What she couldn't yet speak of was the look of love in his eyes and the healing beginning in her heart.

Naomi was still able to see the well, but she was far from it now, and she began to question herself. The whole town was following her. If she were wrong, they would never forget it, just as they never forgot her past. She had taken a chance on so many men. The one with whom she was in relationship now was a slave—a relationship that ensured she would never be like the other women in the town. He treated her better than any other man had. But still he was similar to them. This Jew they were going to see, however, seemed as different from other men as people are from animals.

When Naomi stood before Jesus again, she knelt in acknowledgment of her acceptance of the gift he had shared with her. Then Jesus placed his hands on her head and recited a blessing, causing gasps of surprise in the crowd. *Wasn't he Jewish? Would he touch a Samaritan woman?* The adults encircled Jesus and Naomi more tightly, out of intense curiosity. Some of the smaller children scrambled toward Jesus, causing the mothers and fathers to move in even closer. Jesus squatted down to talk with and say blessings over each one, which relaxed the people and the atmosphere. People even began to whisper cheerfully and laugh. Then Jesus stood up and began to speak to everyone.

Hours later, Jesus, the Twelve, and the townspeople walked back to the village together. Naomi trailed behind them now, quiet and absorbed in the relief and happiness of being right about at least one man in her life. She saw her entire town affirm that Jesus was truly the Savior of the world. She was the first among her people to know it—and to share it.[1]

---

[1] A fictionalized version of John 4:1-42.

Just what was Jesus doing?

This chapter is not just about women who want to evangelize or preach. It is for any woman who feels called to minister on a larger scale (not only to children, teens, or women) or is gifted for general leadership in the church. Church leadership is about working with Jesus. Jesus could have chosen one or all of the male disciples to work with him for this Samaritan revival. But he chose a very unlikely woman instead.

Choosing any woman at all—even the most matronly—as a coworker was countercultural. Keep in mind that in Jesus' day, rabbis were encouraged not to talk with women in public, let alone in private. Having a theological discussion outside with a woman would have been very suspect. Onlookers (such as the twelve men) would have assumed she was a prostitute. Usually, the only women who engaged in philosophical or theological discussion with men were the *hetaerae*, women who provided both sexual favors and intellectual discussion at banquets. In Greco-Roman culture, which influenced the Jewish people, the virtuous woman was a private one. She did not venture out into public places except for religious reasons, and then only accompanied by a female slave. Jesus seemed unconcerned about what the disciples or anyone else might think about him being alone with a woman and sharing with her deep truths about God (for more on men and women coministering, see chapter 8).

He also made a point of showing the woman that he saw her as an equal. First, he asked her for water. In doing so, Jesus was reaching out to her, not as a superior but as someone in need of her hospitality and acceptance. (In Palestine, the act of giving someone water was an act of trust and friendship.) Second, he shared many important truths with her, especially truths about himself, demonstrating that he saw her as spiritually capable. (Common Jewish thought about women's spirituality was that women—because of their spiritual inferiority—did not need to be educated in the Torah or fulfill all religious obligations.) Jesus did not patronize the Samaritan woman, but set the stage for her to be a true coworker.

This is especially amazing given that the Pharisees viewed Samaritan women and all their possessions—from the day of their birth—as they would view a menstruant: unclean.[2] This accounts partly for the woman's surprise when Jesus asked her for water from her vessel. When the disciples arrived, they were likely stymied both by the fact that Rabbi Jesus was

---

[2] There was a history of religious and political conflict between Jews and Samaritans, though they shared a similar ethnic background and religion. Moreover, all non-Jewish women and their possessions were automatically assumed to be "unclean" because they did not follow the proper purifications rites.

talking to a woman of questionable background (because she was alone out in public), and that he would receive water from a Samaritan.

In the eyes of her own culture as well as Jewish culture, something else about this woman made her an unlikely coworker of the Messiah. She had a "past." Actually, the text does not tell us if the woman had been widowed or divorced those five times; it only says that that for some reason, she is now living with a man who is not her husband. It is easy to imagine ways in which she might have endured much pain (being used sexually as a slave; enduring grief from widowhood; facing rejection from others; suffering abuse from husbands; suffering abuse from her mothers-in-law, which was common; dealing with early childhood losses or abuse; and so on).

Regardless, this woman has been seen through history as "loose," and so the power of her ministry with Jesus has been overlooked. Yet, she became one of the first large-scale evangelists as she convinced her whole town to come and see Jesus. He stayed and welcomed the townspeople, and received their welcome to him. These Gentile people then became convinced Jesus was the Messiah, not only because of the woman's word, but also because of knowing him (John 4:39-42). This is the way we all come to Christ now—through the words of humans and through the actual experience of meeting Christ.

Jesus' interaction with this woman challenges the belief that it is a sin for women to minister to the larger body of Christ. Jesus' meeting with the woman at the well was no accident of fate. His reason for choosing her wasn't that no man was available. He had his twelve male disciples with him, but sent them on to the city to get food (John 4:8), and it was food they continued to focus on, despite Jesus' obvious desire to help them see what was going on spiritually (John 4:27-39).

The Samaritan woman was better prepared than the male disciples to introduce her people to Jesus. She had a better sense of what Jesus' mission was about than did the Twelve. The Samaritans viewed the Messiah (they called him *Taheb*, or "Restorer") to be more of a prophet who would usher in a new era, like Moses, and this understanding fit Jesus' mission better. The Jewish people, including the twelve disciples, were expecting the Messiah to be a powerful new ruler, more like King David. Jesus denied this powerful-ruler role and encouraged his disciples to do the same, despite their resistance (see Luke 22). And so to the Twelve, Jesus referred to himself as "Son of Man" (or "Human One") and never as "Christ." But with the Samaritan woman, he conceded that he was the Messiah (John 4:26).

By revealing more of his mission to a woman than to his male disciples, and by choosing her to minister instead of them, he acknowledged women's worth, full humanity, and ability to be his coworkers.[3]

---

[3] She also witnessed in a way more extensive than Philip witnessed to Nathanael, but still in parallel ("'Nazareth! Can anything good come from there?' Nathanael asked. 'Come and see,' said Philip," John 1:46). Additionally, the Samaritan woman ministered on a larger scale than the disciples generally ministered, prior to Pentecost. Many from her town believed because of her testimony and Jesus' visit.

Questions for Reflection/Discussion

1. What "cultural laws" does Jesus break in order to work with the Samaritan woman to bring salvation to the townspeople?

2. What "cultural laws" in our churches make it likely that women will feel as though Christ would never choose them to work with him to minister to the whole church?

3. What do you think of Erline's question: "Pastor Joe, you're saying I can be an evangelist overseas. I can take leadership in explaining all the Scripture passages about Christ to both men and women as long as it's in another culture. I could even preach and help these people grow up in Christ. But I'm just wondering, why is that sinful here? Was I even wrong to bring my male friends to faith in Christ?"

4. What have your experiences been with others' interpretations of 1 Timothy 2:8-12, the passage which briefly came to Erline's mind ("Those verses are in there about women not being in leadership")? (If you would like to know a little more about how to interpret any Bible passage, see Appendix A. For my interpretation of 1 Timothy 2:8-15, read Appendix C).

5. What barriers do you think keep the "Pastor Joes" of the church from being able to believe that God might want to work with women in surprising ways?

Meditation for Healing

Find a place where you can relax. Invite the Holy Spirit to come close and to help you be aware of being in Jesus' presence. (Even if you don't *feel* Jesus' presence, go ahead and affirm that presence.) Think of several of your male friends and acquaintances whom you admire and whom you see as "chosen by God." Picture them with Jesus on a mission to your own city. Jesus sends them on into town to get food, while he goes to a café to meet you. Imagine what kind of conversation he might have with you, to get you to see that he has the ability to quench your spiritual thirst. What do you need convincing of, spiritually? (Perhaps, that Jesus can work with you in any way he chooses?) Now imagine he sends you from there on a mission to do something you thought only your male friends and acquaintances could do—such as show other men and women the way to spiritual refreshment in Christ. If you like to write, write out this story. Or draw it. Or talk out the story in God's presence, or with a close friend.

If you've been told that emotional expression is a weakness...

chapter 4

I felt sure I could break off the ends of the dreadlocks sticking out of my knit hat, if I tried. It was that cold in Illinois in the winter. I was from Southern California! What was I doing here, especially at a *missions* conference? Tromping through the snow, I looked to the conference room doors with longing. I knew warmth waited inside—and maybe boredom. Minutes later, the heavy doors banged shut behind me, sealing me into the room. "Thank God!" I said aloud.

I stopped at the first booth, and the next and the next. I sighed. Every photo showed a smiling missionary or national. Ironically, their smiles reminded me of my dismal experience growing up in the church. In my church, happiness was the only appropriate emotion to express. And you didn't confess your sins. You just didn't sin. If you did, you hid it. Well, I was tired of hiding it. I had sinned aplenty, and I was still hanging on to that nasty nicotine habit—one of the worst sins of all, or so you'd think from the way people looked down their noses at me every time I left a church service for a smoke. But now I was an adult, and I could be true to me.

My belief in Christ was my real problem. I *couldn't* stop believing even though I'd tried, in order to just do away with church entirely. I couldn't even stop wanting others to believe. At twenty years old, I wanted to do something meaningful for God. I knew Christ was for real and that God accepted perpetual sinners like me. But would I ever fit in with other Christians? Could I be a part of any religious organization?

In a corner, a cozy book section beckoned me. Beginning to walk with purpose now, I yanked off my red mittens and stuffed one in each pocket, preparing to escape my gray "left-over-from-church-days" feelings with a good book. I smiled when I spotted a "gender issues" section, remembering that at the conference everyone had been given an "inclusive-language" Bible. This had excited me, because ever since I was a freshman in high school I'd thought the Bible seemed to be addressed mostly to men. But when I'd complained about that to my dad (a deacon), all I got was a cold stare. My dad read nothing but the King James Version, so what did I expect?

Now, as I read the back of a book about women in ministry, I couldn't help overhearing two young men talking beside me.

"I don't think women should be pastors, do you?"

"Nah."

"They're too emotional."

"That's right. Half the time they probably couldn't get through a sermon without crying."

I stood still as I listened, stunned. *I can't believe they just said women are too emotional to be pastors!* I mean, yeah, my dad felt that way—and come to think of it so did my mom and my pastor and nearly everyone at church over thirty—but I thought they were old-fashioned. These guys were *my* age.

Incensed and curious at the same time, I moved closer, still pretending to read the back of my book. The conversation veered into the realm of the anecdotal. One of the young men said, "Yeah. I know this one girl; she cries so often she quit wearing mascara to church."

Over the sound of my pounding heart, I cleared my throat and said as calmly as possible, "Excuse me, but I overheard your conversation. Where in Scripture does God say that emotional expression is *wrong?*"

Their faces turned into blank pages. As one of them put a book back on the shelf, he said, "Oh, well, sorry if we offended you, miss."

They quickly walked away, snickering to one another. The adrenaline rush had filled me with energy but left me aimless. I merged into the crowd, anonymous again.

As I roamed, my thoughts turned into question after question: *Which century am I in? Why do I always have to go around defending my gender? Who do those BOYS think they are, anyway?* My brow creased as the reality of what they had said sunk in. They were only voicing what my own church had modeled for me all my life. Being a good Christian—and especially one strong enough to lead others—meant keeping all sign of weakness, sin, and emotional vulnerability hidden. If women can't or won't do that, then it just proves the point that they are natural followers, a weaker kind of Christian.

Memories began to flash across my mind as I wandered around the huge room, tuning out conversations and mini-video presentations at the booths all around me. I remembered when I was just six years old, I was taunted by an eight-year-old boy for crying in Sunday school because my mother was in the hospital. Our teacher scolded the boy by saying, "She's a *girl*!" That stopped my tears, for the moment. Even at that age I had wondered, *What does crying when you're sad have to do with being a girl?*

I remembered how my youth leader said once that she was glad her husband was the head of the home, because she was too emotional to be trusted with making decisions. I had thought to myself, *I'm a girl. Am I too emotional to make good decisions too?* That was when I first realized—though I could not articulate it then—that the church often perceives self-doubt in a woman as a "virtue" that should be cultivated. I didn't buy it. Maybe that's why I just couldn't fit in—I had too much self-confidence and self-esteem.

It's not like I had great aspirations to church leadership. But I knew that being able to feel and express deep emotions has nothing to do with having an ability to lead others, and could even make you a better leader. Besides, I knew lots of women who follow their heads, not their hearts.

It obviously didn't matter what *I* thought, though. Those boys convinced me that religious organizations and their unfair dogmas are too big for one person to take on.

I was out of there. It was just too cold.

When Jesus caught sight of Martha, he left the circle of men.

They watched him go and occasionally glanced over at him. Jesus stood in front of Martha and waited for her to speak. He knew that she and her sister, Mary, were in deep grief over their brother's death. The sisters loved their brother very deeply. Jesus understood that, because he knew their stories. All they had was each other—no spouses, no children, no parents. Jesus knew they didn't understand why he hadn't come immediately when they had sent him word that Lazarus was gravely ill. God had told Jesus the illness would not lead to death, but they did not know this.

"Lord, if you had been here, my brother would not have died," Martha began. Then she looked down, embarrassed at having nearly rebuked her Teacher.

Jesus fixed his compassionate eyes on hers, waiting.

She finally looked up at him, and ventured a cloaked request. She said, "But I know that even now God will give you whatever you ask."

Jesus spoke with the slow force of a bulb birthing a spring flower: "Your brother will rise again."

"I know he will rise again in the resurrection at the last day," she said, as though this were a consolation prize for a contest she had dearly wanted to win.

Jesus explained, "I am the resurrection and the life. Anyone who believes in me will live, even though they die, and whoever lives by believing in me will never die." He waited for her to lift her eyes to meet his again, then asked, "Do you believe this?"

Jesus talked often with Mary and Martha and their brother about his mission from the Father. They had provided a place for Jesus to unwind after long days with many needy people and overwhelmed disciples. How many meals had they shared together, just talking? Yet he'd never revealed to them that he was the resurrection and the life, until now.

Martha's response gladdened his heart. "Yes, Lord," she told him, "I believe that you are the Messiah, the Son of God, the One coming into the world."

"Where is Mary?" Jesus asked.

Martha said, "I'll be right back," and turned to leave.

Not long afterward, Jesus saw Mary hurrying toward him, with Martha and a crowd of people following right behind. When Mary saw that Jesus was watching her, she slackened her pace. Even from a distance he could see her red and swollen eyes, and his heart ached for her. She fell to her knees before him and her knotted, hoarse throat strained to say, "Lord...if you had been here...my brother would not have died."

Mary seemed to look for an answer in Jesus' eyes, to understand, but he gave no answer. Her face contorted as another shock of grief went through her.

"Where have you laid him?" Jesus finally asked softly.

The mourning women spoke for her, "Come and see, Lord."

Tears began to cloud Jesus' eyes and his throat tightened. If the Father had told him to come earlier, how quickly he would have come. How it hurt him to see his dear friends feeling so abandoned and let down by him. How it angered him that death could have its way like this. The cacophony of moaning and crying overcame him, and his own tears filled his eyes to overflowing.

Mary stopped crying immediately and stared at Jesus. Some of his friends and acquaintances stopped weeping long enough to say to each other, "See how he loved him!" Others, with knowing expressions, whispered behind cupped hands, "Could not he who opened the eyes of the blind man have kept this man from dying?"

Jesus, with his head down, led Mary and Martha and the crowd toward the tomb. When they reached it, he again felt the deep sting of death, overlaid with the hurt of the two sisters' disappointment with him. He gazed soberly at the stone that covered the cave's entrance as though he stared at the gateway to death itself. Tears again welled up as he thought of all the trust Martha and Mary had placed in him over the years, and that they thought he had let them down, when he knew better than any how much their brother meant to them.

"Take away the stone," Jesus said in a broken voice to three men standing nearby.

Martha interjected, "But Lord, by this time there is a bad odor, for he has been there four days." Jesus knew Martha well enough to know she was trying to protect him. She just didn't want to see him shamed, as she thought his status had already been diminished in the eyes of his followers and the other mourners.

Jesus responded to her unspoken thoughts and said, "Did I not tell you that if you believe, you will see the glory of God?"

Martha nodded and blinked her assent, chagrined.

Jesus turned toward the men to remind them of his request, and together they went to one side of the stone and pushed with all their strength to remove it. The women watched the hole in the stone wall appear—and, with it, a sweet but disgusting odor wafted out.

Jesus stood at the entrance as the others backed away, holding their noses and breathing through garments. A soft murmur arose. He looked over his shoulder at the onlookers, and then he looked up as he said,

"Father, I thank you that you have heard me. I knew that you always hear me, but I said this for the benefit of the crowd standing here, so that they may believe that you sent me."

Then he shouted, "Lazarus, come out!" The people gawked at this spectacle. The smell told the story—Lazarus was dead, had been dead for days. Who did this man think he was? They glanced at one another with widened eyes. Then some stepped backward, as if trying to get away from something. A few laughed aloud in unbelief, as they took in the vision before them. It was Lazarus feeling his way up the stairs, dressed as a living dead man, his hands and feet wound with linen, his face covered.

Jesus turned quickly to the sisters and said joyfully, "Unbind him, and let him go." Mary and Martha both took a few steps toward Lazarus, then Mary stopped and Martha ran to him first, pulling off the face cloth so she could see that her brother was all right. When Mary saw his so-familiar almond-shaped brown eyes blinking at the light, she lunged for him, wrapping her arms around him. The grave clothes confined Lazarus, and Mary nearly toppled his small frame right over, but the others caught him. As they pushed him back up, everyone laughed with ecstatic amazement. Jesus laughed too.[1]

---

[1] A fictionalized version of John 11:17-44.

Just what was Jesus doing?

Oftentimes the question of whether women can be effective leaders in the church or elsewhere revolves in part around the belief that women are more emotional than men, which makes them ill-equipped to serve in any leadership capacity. It is thought that women are "touchy-feely," cry too easily, and get their feelings hurt too readily to withstand the strains of leadership.[2] The assumptions are that crying is a sign of personal weakness, and that it is a weakness men should avoid because it is a "woman's weakness." In a way, crying is part of the "virtue of self-doubt" that women are expected to display. A woman's tears confirm to her and to everyone else her supposed emotional and even intellectual fragility.

Both men and women are guilty of holding these beliefs and assumptions, and both suffer as a result. Women refrain from voicing strong opinions and feelings in public settings because of the fear that they will be seen as irrational. Men, taught to suppress their vulnerable emotions from an early age in order to be "manly" rather than "like a girl," may find it challenging to even identify what they are feeling, and may find that anger is the only emotion they are comfortable expressing.

---

[2] Women's *angry* feelings, however, are generally not acknowledged, and if they are, it is by labeling the woman a "bitch."

As the perfect reflection of God (Hebrews 1:3; 2 Corinthians 4:4; Colossians 1:15) Jesus confronted our culture's assumptions about emotional expression and gender through his example in this story about Martha, Mary, and Lazarus. He challenged the belief that vulnerable emotional expression is a sign of shameful weakness by openly weeping himself. The almighty God cries sometimes! His sadness over the death of his friend Lazarus prompted him to participate in the Jewish tradition of mourning openly over a death. Women rather than men were traditional paid mourners, yet Jesus spontaneously wept with the women. And this is not the only time he expressed profound grief. In Luke 19:41-44 we see him weeping, in front of his disciples, over the people of Jerusalem; Matthew 26:38 records Jesus saying he was "overwhelmed with sorrow" in the Garden of Gethsemane; Hebrews 5:7 notes that "During the days of Jesus' life on earth, he offered up prayers and petitions with fervent cries and tears to the one who could save him from death." If the Son of God expressed his vulnerable emotions through tears, can it really be so shameful?

By weeping openly, Jesus inadvertently confronted the stereotype that women are more emotional than men. Martha, in contrast, did not weep. In fact, she remained relatively unemotional during the entire drama. She entreated

Jesus diplomatically for a miracle (John 11:21-22); discussed theological matters in a way parallel to Peter's confession of Christ (John 11:27 and 6:68-69; compare to Peter in Luke 9:20); and then thought practically about her brother's death in reminding Jesus of the stench in the tomb (John 11:39). So although it was likely unintentional, John has illustrated for us a "stereotype reversal." This is true-to-life, however, as we all could give examples of women and men who do not fit gender stereotypes regarding emotional expression.[3]

Jesus is the ultimate example of someone who was "okay" with his and others' emotions, whether those of men or women. He could handle Mary's and Martha's anger toward him just as well as their sadness. In fact, he was rebuked in the same way by Mary *and* Martha. They both said to him, "Lord if you had been here, my brother would not have died" (John 11:21, 32). But Jesus responded not with defensiveness, as he might have done (a pious rabbi being nearly rebuked by two women in public), but with compassionate tears. Instead of trying to protect his own self-image, or labeling the women in

---

[3] Psychological researchers have been addressing the questions concerning the differing emotional expressiveness of women and men. If you are interested, take a look at the reviews of the research in the book *Gender and Emotion: Social Psychological Perspectives* (New York: Cambridge University Press, 2000), edited by Agneta H. Fischer.

negative way, Jesus sided with the women against death, felt its pang with them, and took it away!

It's no wonder Jesus took on the title "Human One" (often translated "Son of Man"). Jesus was comfortable with the full range of feelings that come with our humanity, was strong enough to appear "weak," and implicitly invited men and women alike to follow his example.

Questions for Reflection/Discussion

1. What do you think Jesus would say to the young woman in the first story? What would he say to the two young men?

2. If Jesus were a pastor or religious leader living in our society, what "cultural laws" would he be breaking by weeping openly?

3. What do you think God thinks about the expression of tender emotions? Is God concerned about men and/or religious leaders not revealing their human vulnerability? Reflect on the reasons for your answer.

4. Sometimes we can accept women's sadness as being "typical," but reject women's anger. (Angry women, for example, get called names.) What did you think about the young woman's anger? Was it justified? Why or why not? Based on Jesus' response to Mary's and Martha's anger, how do you think Jesus would handle the young woman's anger?

Meditation for Healing

Find a place where you can relax. Invite the Holy Spirit to come close and to help you be aware of being in Jesus' presence. (Even if you don't *feel* Jesus' presence, go ahead and affirm that presence.) Remember a time when you felt embarrassed over your emotional response to something, especially if it included a sense of shame for being "an emotional woman." Or call to mind a time when you felt angry over an accusation of women being "too emotional." Then imagine Jesus in either situation with you. What expression does he have on his face? What is Jesus feeling in identification with you? How do your feelings affect his? How does he feel about your feelings of hurt or anger, shame or grief, and so on? Imagine what Jesus might say to you; consider writing these words to yourself in a letter. What might he do for you? Would he remind you of some truth about himself or others, or would he just cry with you or feel anger as you do, or both?

Talk it out with Jesus in prayer, or pray it through with a trusted friend or mentor.

And/Or. Remember a time when you felt immensely disappointed with Jesus. You thought he would heal someone or stop an abusive situation, and he did not. Recalling Jesus' emotional response to Mary's hurt, write out, talk out to God in prayer, or talk out with a friend how Jesus might feel about your disappointment. Then see if you can find any sign of "resurrection" in the situation, any sign of God bringing about healing or restoration or new life. It may not be there right now, but look for it, asking God to open your eyes to what God is doing. Then meditate on the statement, "I am the resurrection and the life. Anyone who believes in me, will live, even though they die; and whoever lives by believing in me will never die" (John 11:25-26). Ask God to show you what this means for you and those you care about.

If church has been an unsafe place to share your woundedness...

chapter 5

I heard that smelling a cut lemon could calm you down if you were nervous. I'm not an idiot, so I took my lemon into a church bathroom stall. Someone said, "Wow, that's powerful smelling toilet-bowl cleaner," as she walked out, and I smiled. I just couldn't believe I'd said yes to speaking to my youth group about my testimony. Dumb, dumb, dumb. But after smelling the lemon I did feel a little more relaxed, so I put it back into my purse, gathered my things and walked out.

As I reviewed my notes a few minutes later, I realized I *was* excited to tell these guys about the things Jesus had done in my life since I had become a Christian two years ago at youth camp. Yet, I dreaded that they might ask me questions about my family. I wanted to tell the truth, but not the whole truth. It's just that these kids seemed so...good. They came from good homes with good parents. Maybe they could understand some things, but, about my father? No way. That's why I'd decided not to even mention him.

When Sylvia, our youth leader, introduced me, I took a deep breath and started in. "All my life I had wondered if I was really loved." Then I listed all the ways I had tried to feel loved and to feel that I belonged: eating too much to try to feel comforted, starving myself in an effort to look good for the guys, taking drugs to have a good time with my friends and to forget my feelings of loneliness. And always wearing black. It fit my mood: I'd thought often about death, even suicide.

I wasn't eager to tell people why I'd been so messed up. So I kind of cut and pasted my life story. My parents divorced, we moved around a lot. My brother and I basically raised each other, because my mom was working two jobs. But then as soon as my brother could work, he was gone all the time too. I was depressed and lonely a lot—well, except when I was with my other friends who were depressed and lonely.

Jesus changed all that. Some people get all excited about feeling forgiven, but for me it was especially exciting to know that I was loved. Not just by Jesus, but also by the people at camp. Coming back was harder, because I didn't really know the people I'd gone to camp with, and I had to get used to church and the way they do things. But I was more than willing. I got rid of my eyebrow ring because I knew that weirded some people out, and I quit wearing black all the time, and I even stopped smoking marijuana. I just didn't need it anymore; that old pain deep inside was mostly gone.

When I finished speaking, Sylvia asked if anyone in the group had questions for me.

Silence.

Just when I thought I might be off the hook, Lottie, a tenth-grader who was a year behind me, pushed her glasses up on her nose and said, "Um, Marti, you didn't mention your father. Where was he when you were growing up? Do you see him now?"

"Oh, well, not really..." I trailed off.

"I mean, like, I know you said your parents were divorced, but do you see your dad at all now?" She chewed her gum vigorously, waiting.

I could hear the fidgeting in the background as I tried to figure out what to say. I looked at Sylvia, wondering if she might get me out of this, but she tilted her head to the side and seemed like she was waiting to hear too. Everyone stared at me as if I was providing the evening's media entertainment. I almost blurted it out: "He's in jail. For molesting me." But in one last effort to protect myself, I said, "Um, I really don't see my dad at all any more."

"Oh, yeah, I understand," Lottie said.

I felt myself sinking. I knew she didn't understand. She'd grown up in the church all her life and had two loving parents, and a white picket fence around her perfect, tract home where she'd always lived. Panicking, I prayed, *Please don't let them ask any questions.* I laughed

» *if church has been unsafe* « 79

and folded my hands in my lap, hoping it would all be over soon, burying the shame I felt over the unspoken truth about my life.

Sylvia said, "Thanks, Marti, that was great. God's done some awesome things in your life," as she squinted her eyes up in what looked to me like fake sincerity.

"Any time," I said, and smiled as though I were in the light of the forgiving twilight sun instead of the exposing fluorescent. *Thank God*, I thought, *No one ever has to know.*

The crowd moved like a river following after Jesus and Jairus. The well-respected synagogue leader had pled with Jesus to come to his house and heal his daughter, who was dying, and Jesus had agreed to do so.

A woman pursued the group at a distance. She had suffered a continual flow of blood for twelve years now, and had worked carefully to keep this a secret, because she did not want to be known as the woman who was "perpetually unclean." Her family knew, however, and had little to do with her. People often wondered why she was alone, why her husband had left town so many years ago, and why she had not remarried, as was customary.

They whispered to each other that she must be barren, with a cursed womb. Or maybe she was simply cursed.

The woman noticed the crowd; she recognized some of the same diseased, blind, deaf, and crippled people she often saw in her daily efforts to get alms on which to live. One advantage of her particular ailment was that she could not earn money through prostitution. She was afraid she might have been tempted to do this otherwise, because many days she went hungry.

As she drew closer, she heard people crying out, "Rabbi!" and "Jesus!" but she could not see who they were calling to. She realized, however, this man must be the one she had heard people talking about—the one they said could heal people by the power of God.

She paused for a moment. She had to get to Jesus! But talking to him was out of the question. As desperate as she was, she couldn't imagine herself telling anyone her shameful secret. There had to be some other way to receive his healing. She thought, *If I just get close enough to touch even the hem of his garment, I will be healed.*

She pushed her way between the sweaty, smelly men and women, flinching at the intimacy of contact she did not want. Some stood in her way or elbowed her in their attempts to keep her from getting past them.

It was easy to identify Jesus once she entered the center of the crowd. He wore a rabbinic turban. Yet his ordinariness surprised her and comforted her. Fixing her gaze on his drab, slightly worn-out cloak, she finally was able to reach around the knees of an old, crippled man stooped directly behind Jesus, and touch that rough cloth. At that moment—just as she had believed would happen—her bleeding stopped.

But then to her horror, Jesus paused, and so did the synagogue leader and the crowd. The people drew even tighter around Jesus, straining to make eye contact with him and calling out to him. The woman crouched behind the elderly man as Jesus asked loudly, "Who touched me?"

Peter called out to Jesus with a hint of incredulity in his voice, "Master, the people are crowding and pressing against you." Jesus ignored him and looked around into the seeking eyes of the people, many of them strangers. "Someone touched me, for I know that power has gone out from me," he persisted. Jesus was not going anywhere until he had an answer. As he scanned the people's faces, they stared back at him. Who had touched Jesus? Why did it matter? Was he going to the temple and feared someone had made him unclean?

Then all around her, eyes began to focus upon the woman trying to hide from Jesus. *Why am I hiding?* she asked herself. *I am well! I am clean!* Yet she trembled before the reality of such power. With a sudden understanding of her new position in life, she stood up and made her way to Jesus, then fell down in front of him with a sense of awe. Looking down at the hem of his garment, she said: "Lord, I'm the one who touched you, and I was healed!"

"Yes, you are the one," Jesus said.

"I was very sick, Rabbi," she said. He waited for her to continue. As she looked into his face, she no longer felt the cold, curious stares of those around her, because this gentle rabbi was listening.

She spoke softly, but those around her quieted in order to hear. "When I was twelve," she began, "I started bleeding all the time. And passing out. In the market with my mother, or even just playing with friends. It scared me. I told my mother, and she told me not to tell anyone else. And then, when I turned fourteen, my father suddenly said I had to leave the family because I was a disgrace. I was no longer his daughter. I think he was afraid word would get out, and that I could never marry. But then my father quickly arranged for a much older man to marry me. Yet this man left me when he discovered my illness. He wasn't cruel; he gave me some money. I spent all I had on doctors, who could do nothing but give me 'remedies' that made me suffer even more. But this morning I woke up with real sense of hope, I think because I had heard about you. I knew when I saw you that if I could just touch your cloak, I could begin to live. Thank you."

Jesus looked her in the eye and said, "Daughter, your faith has healed you. Go in peace." The crowd, which had seemed so cold to her before, erupted in cheers and thanks to God. They believed her story and accepted that she was now "clean."

As she parted for that moment—for she would return to follow Jesus—the words "Daughter, your faith has made you well," reverberated in her ears. Peace and joy were filling her like the people filled every space around Jesus. She had revealed the secret of her shame-stricken life to this holy man, and he had called her daughter—in front of everyone![1]

---

[1] A fictionalized version of Luke 8:40-48.

> ## *Just what was Jesus doing?*
>
> Many people in the church, both women and men, keep secrets due to a sense of shame. We are afraid to tell anyone our secrets because we don't feel safe. We fear being judged or labeled, and sometimes rightly so.
>
> Sometimes these "shameful" secrets aren't really shameful, as was the case with the woman in this Gospel story. This woman could not help her physical illness, nor can those who have a mental illness or those who have been harmed through sexual or physical abuse, rape, spousal abuse, or their husband's adultery. Other times, past or present sins make us feel we need to keep secrets from people in the church.
>
> Due to our cultural values, Christians tend to judge some weaknesses and sins as more offensive than others. For example, few in the North Ameri-

can church seem bothered by others being greedy. In fact, greed is hardly even recognized, since it is a sin which we share as a culture. (Yet, note Paul's take on greed: 1 Corinthians 5:11; 1 Corinthians 6:10; Ephesians 5:5; 1 Timothy 3:8; Titus 1:7; Colossians 3:5; 1 Thessalonians 2:5). Those of us who tend toward greed, however, may still get very upset about someone else's tendency toward homosexuality.

If we have been unfairly labeled in the church due to our or someone else's sin or weakness, then we may feel a sense of shame and a need to keep secrets. Yet, if someone truly understood our story, he or she would likely demonstrate grace and love for us, just as Christ did for the woman with the hemorrhage.

In order to love this unnamed "unclean" woman, Jesus did some rather remarkable things within his culture. He was completely unconcerned with the woman's "uncleanness" and that she touched him while still "unclean," temporarily imparting that status to him.[2] Yet, this was no small matter for Jews and Jewish teachers. In

---

[2] Being "unclean" was not the same as having sinned, and could be remedied through both time and purification rites. Nonetheless, great pains were taken, when possible, to avoid being unclean. Men were not to have sexual relations with their wives during their menstrual periods, for example (this act *would* be considered sinful), and women were to avoid "tempting" their husbands sexually during that time as well. The reasons for all the religious rules surrounding menstruation are unclear. (There were similar clean/unclean designations relating to a corpse, to anyone with skin diseases, and to a man having emitted semen).

Jesus' day, menstruation was not clearly understood as being biologically necessary for procreation. It was seen as an abomination, a part of the punishment given to Eve due to the sin in Eden. The Pharisaic writings concerned themselves in great detail with menstruation and purity laws, due to men's and women's desire to avoid "uncleanness." Jesus appeared unconcerned with being made "unclean"—his concern was with the woman herself.

Another notable aspect of this story is that when we meet this woman, Jesus was in the middle of helping a well-respected synagogue ruler named Jairus. But as soon as Jesus realized power had left him due to someone's faith, he immediately stopped what he was doing for the ruler, despite the man's urgency concerning his daughter. Jairus and the woman lived at opposite ends of the social spectrum. In contrast to Jairus, who was wealthy and influential, the woman was nameless and probably divorced or never married—powerless. We do not know for sure if she was a Jew or Gentile. What money she had, she had spent on doctors, and so she was poor. The cultural tendency of religious leaders may have been to rush to help those with power, but Jesus did not do this (and he certainly criticized the Pharisees for this propensity); Jesus was willing to be interrupted by a poor and isolated woman.

Jesus was too strong to let cultural and religious laws keep him from loving someone in need. The woman took a risk on Jesus, and found he was a safe person, so safe that she did not have to experience shame in any way with him. His power and love allowed her to only touch his clothing, without having to reveal her illness, and the source of her shame vanished.

Then, without prompting, "in the presence of all the people, she told why she had touched him" (Luke 8:47), even though she had at first come "trembling" to him. It seems that once she stood face-to-face with Jesus, she knew she had nothing to fear. She could tell her story.

The woman recognized Jesus as loving and powerful, and Jesus, likewise, saw in the woman something *he* valued highly: faith. Indeed, Jesus attributed her healing to *her* faith, not to his power, and he gave her a new label: *Daughter*.

Jesus longs to give *you* a new name, as well.

Questions for Reflection/Discussion:

1. Did you, in any way, relate to Marti or the woman with the hemorrhage? What memories did their stories bring to mind for you?

2. Marti did not feel safe telling others about the things that had happened to her that caused her to feel shame. What "cultural laws" sometimes make the church an unsafe place to reveal wounds or sins?

3. What does the Gospel story tell you about what Jesus values in people?

4. What might have happened if the nameless woman had not trusted Jesus enough to risk touching his cloak? In what small way could you take a risk on Jesus, in order to begin to be healed from shame?

Meditation for Healing

If there is a secret hurt or sin in your past that you feel has "labeled" you, find someone you trust with whom to share your story. Ask this person ahead of time to help you listen together for the new names Jesus has for you, to replace the labels that you or society has given you. (For instance, you may hear Precious Daughter instead of Fornicator; or Noble, Courageous One, instead of Divorced Woman.)

You may not have anyone you feel you can trust now. Ask Jesus to bring a trustworthy person to you. In the meantime, keep your eyes open for his answer. Just like the woman came "trembling" to the feet of Jesus, you may be scared to tell your story. Push ahead anyway, "through the crowd," and trust that Jesus has healing power and a new name for you. You can listen for his voice calling out your new name, even now. What is Jesus saying?

If, as a single woman, your gifts have been rejected or overlooked...

chapter 6

"Your graduate degrees mean nothing here—without the covering of a husband, anyway," the pastor said, leaning back in his chair. Then, more softly, "We do, however, have a need for a secretary."

A large boulder lodged itself in my stomach. I half-expected to be turned down, but I wasn't expecting *this*—secretarial work? It was true, I had already noticed, that only married women were leaders in the church, and they spoke much to other women about female submission and male headship. So, despite my Masters of Theology (and I knew the bit about the "covering of a husband" was poor exegesis of 1 Corinthians 11, but I kept that to myself), I hadn't asked to teach the Bible. I had asked to teach a session at the leadership retreat on how to lead small groups. I said I had done such a seminar many times in my workplace and had studied the topic in graduate school. But it seemed that I had offended the pastor personally by asking such a thing.

I took a deep breath. "Well, I doubt I would make a good administrative assistant," I said, purposely changing his wording from "secretary." "In fact, I have my own administrative assistant to help me with clerical work," I said.

"Okay, well, if you know someone, pass the word along," he said, and smiled briefly. He then started shuffling through papers on his desk.

"Sure," I said, lingering, hoping the conversation might take a different turn if I just waited.

"Um, Kristi? Could you get me a cup of coffee on your way out?" he asked. He held eye contact with me.

I knew he was testing me, but I didn't care. At that point I just wanted out of his office, so I said, "I'm sorry, but I've got to be going," and got up to leave.

As I got to the door, he said, "Women like you need to learn to serve, Kristi."

I looked at his smug expression, took another deep breath, and walked out. At that moment, I was angry enough I could have blasted him.

But I was also crushed. I had come to the pastor offering my gifts for service. I had already spent years in the church and seen teenage boys asked to do things I was never even considered for, such as preach on a Sunday morning or help with communion. It was simply because of my gender and—it had never been clearer than today—because of my marital status. I was single—and even worse, happy to be single. Except in my church, of course.

What few knew is that I actually feel *called* to singleness. I am passionate about my relationship with God and grateful for all the time I can spend with Jesus in prayer, in worship, and in study. I wanted to serve God by offering my gifts to the church—gifts it didn't seem to want, like the knowledge and skills from my master's degrees in theology and in industrial organizational psychology. I had a good enough job in human resources. But I knew I was called to serve God in the church too.

I didn't talk with most people about my calling to singleness, because few understood it and most distrusted it. When I told my professor in Bible college about it, she dismissed the idea. I was so *young*, she'd said, and wouldn't I miss the *joys* of childbearing and nursing babies? For the last ten years, people who don't know me that well often asked me, on a Sunday morning during the break, "So why are you still single?" or "If you're looking for a matchmaker" (and they'd giggle), "I know this divorced guy—his wife left him with three little ones, can you believe it? And I think he's dating again...." It seemed like families didn't even trust me around their children, like I was weird because I wasn't married by now.

I could ignore the little barbs and insults. But the pastor had backed me against a wall.

I'd always been a strong woman, but never considered myself a feminist. I guess I just hadn't "gone there," as I knew such a stance would make me even more suspect in the eyes of my fellow Christians. But regardless of what position I took about women's issues, I knew that with my gifts I could not spend the rest of my life just sitting in a pew or getting coffee for the pastor.

I also knew there were places that would accept my calling and giftings to a far greater extent. Perhaps I would convert to Orthodoxy or Catholicism, where a calling to singleness is understood. Whatever I did, I would not spend the rest of my life having my gifts rejected in the evangelical church.

Surprise silenced the religious leaders as the woman appeared at the doorway, weeping.

The two men reclining at right angles to Jesus rose up on their elbows to get a look at her as she approached Jesus' ivory inlaid couch. They stared at the unveiled features of her face—reddened, brown eyes; a strong chin; high cheekbones; and small nose. Her raven-black hair hung all around her shoulders. Tear after tear dropped on Jesus' feet as she sobbed without restraint. Jesus waited.

The fresh wheat bread and stew that had been served was growing lukewarm. Some of the men resumed their eating and talking, trying to ignore the woman. One finally sat up as though to tell her to leave, but he lay back down when Jesus narrowed his eyes at him. As the woman bent down and wiped Jesus' feet with her long, tangled hair, all the men in the room but one watched in horror. Jesus waited, as he knew the woman was not finished giving her gifts, the first of which were her tears.

She kissed his feet again and again and then turned over a white perfume bottle, splashing a sweet but mellow fragrance all over them. Jesus deeply breathed in the fragrance. The other men made faces, as though it were a stench. When Simon, the Pharisee who had invited Jesus to have dinner at his house, saw Jesus openly enjoying the perfume and attention this woman bestowed upon him, he stood up angrily, saying to himself, *If this man were a prophet, he would have known who is touching him and what kind of woman she is—that she is a sinner.*

Jesus, still reclining, finally spoke. "Simon, I have something to tell you."

"Tell me, teacher" Simon said briskly. Regaining his composure he slowly relaxed back on to the couch once again.

The room had gone completely quiet. The guests listened eagerly, wanting to hear every word so they could be sure to tell their friends and families about how this supposed rabbi had taught at a banquet in the presence of a prostitute, for they assumed she was such.

"Two people owed money to a certain moneylender. One owed him five hundred denarii, and the other fifty. Neither of them had money to pay him back, so he forgave the debts of both. Now which of them will love him more?"

Simon paused, pursed his lips, and said slowly, "I suppose...the one who had the bigger debt forgiven."

Jesus nodded, expressionless, and said, "You have judged correctly."

Simon smiled with pleasure at Jesus' affirmation of his answer.

Then Jesus turned his head in the direction of the woman. Raising his voice slightly for all to hear, he said to Simon, "Do you see this woman? I came into your house. You did not give me any water for my feet, but she wet my feet with her tears and wiped them with her hair. You did not give me a kiss, but this woman, from the time I entered, has not stopped kissing my feet. You did not put oil on my head, but she has poured perfume on my feet. Therefore, I tell you, her many sins have been forgiven—as her great love has shown. But whoever has been forgiven little loves little."

Then Jesus turned to look at the now quiet woman—who was looking down at the floor to hide the joy she felt at his words—and said, "Your sins are forgiven."

A murmur arose as the offended guests asked each other, "Who is this who even forgives sins?"

Jesus continued to see only the woman. He breathed in the perfume once again before saying, "Your faith has saved you. Go in peace."[1]

---

[1] A fictionalized version of Luke 7:36-50.

Just what was Jesus doing?

Unmarried women often stand on the outside of a church's inner circle, waiting to be "normalized" by marriage and family in the eyes of the "insiders"—married people with children. The gifts single women have to offer may be rejected, not only because they are women, but because they are not "normal"—again, married with children. The older the woman, the more deeply this attitude can be held. Even if their gifts are received, they may still feel looked upon as "unfortunate" or "not blessed."

Married women can also have their gifts rejected, of course, for different reasons. Perhaps they stand in the shadow of a gifted husband (see the second Meditation for Healing in this chapter for more on their unique situations). Even today, in a culture that claims to be far more egalitarian than the Greco-Roman one, the single woman starts out with a lower status in the church than does the married woman. And the woman in this Gospel story, with a "tainted gift," was single, as evidenced by her lack of a head covering.

In the Roman Empire, a single woman without extended family was a "nobody." She had no male sponsor to give her his reflected honor and no source of income except prostitution or begging. A woman in her own right had no honor at all, and honor was very important in Greco-Roman society. The men attending this banquet were very concerned about honor; giving a banquet, and being invited to one, increased one's honor. Simon should have invited Jesus to his house because he saw Jesus as an equal, but the lack of honor he gave the rabbi proved telling—he did not provide for Jesus the very basic rituals of hospitality offered an equal. The disdained woman's love for Jesus was a sharp contrast to Simon's attitude toward Jesus, providing a "teaching moment."

In Jesus' day, banquets were often settings for moral instruction. (We know the setting of Luke 7:36-50 is a banquet because people were reclining on couches, rather than sitting.) Respectable married women were typically not invited to the "symposium" or teaching that followed the meal. If a woman was at a banquet during such a symposium, her very presence would have given her the reputation of a prostitute, because *heterae* (courtesans who also engaged in intellectual discussion) were invited to Greco-Roman banquets. Simon and his guests likely felt uncomfortable and tense due to this woman's unconventional behavior. No religious leader would have wanted to have it said there was a prostitute at the banquet he attended.

The woman's loose hair would have confirmed their suspicions of her, because in that culture it indicated she was a "loose" woman. She may also have been non-Jewish—as evidence suggests there were not many Jewish prostitutes—and if so, she and her possessions would be assumed "unclean." So due to her gender, low status, possibly her foreignness, her presumed lifestyle, and her assertive intrusion into the banquet, the men frowned upon the woman and the gift she brought Jesus. They would have seen her gift of perfume as suspect in more than one way—not only as an "unclean" possession (if she were foreign), but also as bought with immoral earnings and used to attract men looking for sex.

Yet, knowing all this, Jesus accepted her gift wholeheartedly, without reservation. He understood the justice issues behind her "prostitution": Female slaves were expected to be sexually available to all males, and the only freewomen who became prostitutes were those with no extended family for economic support. Jesus did not say to her, "Go and sin no more," because he knew that within her society, she had few options. He had no comment upon her lifestyle, only an offer of forgiveness, affirmation for her faith, a blessing of peace, and public praise for her great love for Jesus.

Jesus' actions couldn't have been more countercultural or controversial. Not only had he—a rabbi, with the reputation of a prophet like the ones of old—received the tainted gift of a "loose" woman, but he had also forgiven her without her having to go through the temple system of sacrifice. Jesus even attributed her salvation to her own faith. Jesus' standards were not like those of most of the religious leaders around him then, and that is still true today.

The following chart is a direct comparison of Simon and the woman who offered her gift to Jesus. When we remember Jesus' values from elsewhere in the Gospels (see especially the Sermon on the Mount in Matthew 5), it becomes clear why Jesus chose this woman as a role model.

Simon	**The Woman**
A. Social Status	
Male (powerful status)	Female (subordinate status)
Pharisee ("separated one")	"Who lived a sinful life" (Luke 7:37)
Host in his own home	Uninvited intruder
Knew the law	Likely had not studied the Torah
Interested in Jesus but suspicious	Passionate about Jesus
Probably well-fed	Probably poor
Probably "clean"	Possibly "unclean"
B. Responses to Jesus	
Invited Jesus to come to him	Took a personal risk to come to Jesus
Judged Jesus	Loved Jesus extravagantly
Inhospitable and proud	Gave an expensive gift, humbled self
Did not fulfill customary obligations of a host	Gave him kisses, washed his feet
"Judged correctly" (Luke 7:43)	Judged correctly about *Jesus*
Defended, well-guarded	Trusted and worshiped Jesus openly

C. Jesus' Responses

Read Simon's thoughts	Turned toward her
Told him about the debtors	Said, "Your sins are forgiven."
Told him, "You have judged correctly"	Told her, "Your faith has saved you; go in peace"
Negatively compared him to the woman, thereby shaming him publicly	Praised her in comparison to the Pharisee, thereby honoring her publicly

In this Gospel account, Jesus set a precedent for elevating the status of single (and married) women and receiving their gifts. No wonder the early church had a countercultural view of women. Jesus' acceptance of the gift of a woman like this one indicates what Jesus showed us all along: He looks at what's inside a person, not at gender, marital status, lifestyle, or ethnicity—and receives the gift accordingly (see Matthew 23:1-36; Luke 11:37-54).

Questions for Reflection/Discussion

1. What parallels do you see between Kristi and the woman with the gift of perfume?

2. Given what you know about Jesus' response to Simon the Pharisee, if Jesus had observed the pastor's attitude toward Kristi, what might Jesus do and say?

3. Imagine Jesus saying to someone like Kristi, "It's too bad you don't like to do the things the church has designated for women to do, and no, you cannot use your knowledge and teaching skills to build up the whole church. You are a woman. And on top of that, you are single, approaching middle age, and childless. That's a little too weird." (Note that Jesus was also single, middle-aged in his culture, and childless!) Reflect on the reasons it is difficult to imagine Jesus saying or thinking such a thing.

4. What "cultural laws" does Jesus break in order to return the love of the woman who demonstrated her gratefulness and adoration through the gifts of her tears and her perfume?

5. What "cultural laws" make it difficult for the church today to love single women and receive the full range of their gifts?

Meditation for Healing

For Single Women: If you are single and have been discriminated against in either subtle or overt ways by other Christians, you probably need an extra dose of Jesus' love. Find a place where you can relax. Invite the Holy Spirit to come close and to help you be aware of being in Jesus' presence. (Even if you don't *feel* Jesus' presence, go ahead and affirm it.) Use whatever medium (writing, drawing, picturing in your mind, singing) works for you to envision the following scene: You are the woman in the Gospel story, "intruding" upon the banquet of "church service." What you have to offer is not an alabaster jar of perfume, but rather your particular gifting (worship leading, teaching, writing, and so on). This gifting can be *symbolized*, however, by the perfume on Jesus' feet. You offer him this gift because you are so grateful to Jesus for forgiving you your sins. Jesus shows you visibly and tells you—even in the presence of those who ignore you or put you down—how much your gift pleases him. In the end, you, and not those around you who may differ from you both in status and in their willingness to love, become the model for Christian service.

For Married Women: If you are a married woman, you can experience just as much discrimination as single women when it comes to what people are willing to accept about your gifts and what people say about how you can use them. If you can make beautiful quilts, for example, but you are also qualified to preach and teach,

» *rejected or overlooked gifts* «

your quilt making will be seen as your special gift because that fits the stereotypical image of a gifted Christian wife. Or perhaps you are not *seen* at all because your husband's gifts are "larger than life." You are standing in his big shadow. Or perhaps you are simply not seen because you are someone's "wife" and not a man. Over time, this sort of invisibility can destroy your self-image, leading you to believe that you really don't matter in comparison to your husband. You become "okay" with the situation and also less than you really are.

Jesus understands and wants to help you know how loved and valued you are, and that he is grieved that the church does not see you as the unique, powerful, gifted servant of God that you are or could be. Find a place where you can relax. Invite the Holy Spirit to come close and to help you be aware of being in Jesus' presence. (Even if you don't *feel* Jesus' presence, go ahead and affirm it.) Use whatever medium (writing, drawing, picturing in your mind, singing) works for you to envision the following scene: You are the woman in the Gospel story, "intruding" upon the banquet of "church service." But you have come to the banquet with your husband. The men greet him with traditional acts of hospitality. Your presence and gift, however, is not welcome, and the religious men act as though you are not present. What you have to offer is not an alabaster jar of perfume, but rather your particular gifting (worship leading, teaching, writing, and so on). This gifting can be *symbolized*, however, by the perfume on

Jesus' feet. You offer this gift to Jesus anyway, because you are so grateful to him for forgiving you your sins. Jesus shows you visibly and tells you, even in the presence of those who ignore you or put you down, how much your gift pleases him. You, in the end, become the model for Christian service. Even though your husband may also be a good servant of Christ, what Jesus wants to point out is the contrast of your love for Jesus and the attitudes of those who did not acknowledge or receive you and your gifts, but treated you as if only your husband's gifts mattered.

If you've felt controlled by the misuse of Scriptures on submission...

chapter 7

Shau-Pei watched her husband put on his tie, and said gently, "I wonder if...I wonder if it might be possible...we miss you at night, my husband."

Man-Wei was spending so many hours, late into the night, at his law office that Shau-Pei felt like a single mother.

Her husband glanced at her. "And so?" he said, stony-faced, loosening the satin against his throat.

"Could you come home earlier some nights, just now and again? We would like to see you more often."

The flash of rage in his eyes caused Shau-Pei to recall, again, that dark day, five years before, in the second year of their marriage. It had been early evening, and she could still remember how the setting sun had made the gold edge on the vase shimmer. She also recalled the full feeling of having a strong opinion, a new experience for her.

As she was serving tea to her husband, she had said. "No, Man-Wei, I don't believe the Chinese government has the right to dictate how many children a family can have. Do you really think Romans 13 applies there, to obey authorities instead of to obey God?"

He had not bothered replying, but instead spoke with the strong voice of one hand across her face.

Now, sitting down on the white bed covers and allowing herself to be comforted by their softness, Shau-Pei glanced at her frightened reflection in the mirror and then quickly looked away. Out of the corner of her eye, she watched Man-Wei walk to the mahogany nightstand on his side of the bed and pick up the King James Bible, given to them at their wedding.

"Do I have to remind you?" he said, holding the black, leather-covered book out to her.

"No need," she said softly, turning her head slightly toward him. "I remember well."

Shau-Pei had only been in America four years when they met, her husband for three. She attended church and had been learning about the roots of radical Christianity. Man-Wei attended as well, but his patriotism remained untouched by what he learned.

To her surprise, Shau-Pei had found her own heart hungrily eating all that it could every Sunday morning. As she swept the porch or shaped wontons, she thought about Jesus' death on the cross, about Jesus' forgiveness of the criminal who hung next to him, about Jesus washing his followers' feet, and about Jesus cooking fish for his followers for breakfast. Scripture was becoming a part of her experience; it was no longer just words, but also images, sounds, smells, and feelings. No one had ever asked her if she wanted Christ to come into her heart. Shau-Pei had not yet known what that meant; but Jesus had responded to her love for him and come anyway.

Now she got up quickly as Man-Wei picked up his briefcase. She made her way to the kitchen, where she sprinkled some blue cleaning powder into the sink and began to scrub as if it were actually dirty. She washed away the blue suds, hoping the tightness in her throat would dissipate as well. She began reorganizing the rice bowls in the cupboard, and restacking matching china bowls, sauce plates, and soup spoons.

As Shau-Pei heard the garage door closing, signaling her husband's departure, tears came to her eyes. "God, why can't I simply say what I want to him?" she whispered. In the five years since that frightening day, she had not allowed herself more than one or two silent tears. But today Man-Wei had come close to hitting her again because of the simple request that he spend more time at home.

He is a good man, a hard working man, she said to herself. *I do not want to make him sink so low again.* But the tears would not stop flowing as she leaned against the kitchen counter, trying to steady herself. She did not know why she was this upset. Afraid her son would come in and see her crying, Shau-Pei quietly walked into her bedroom. She threw herself on the bed and whispered, *Oh, my Lord, make me a better wife! Help me submit like I am supposed to, Jesus, and keep my desires to myself. Please forgive me. I love you.*

Peace like a still, deep lake filled her sorrow-racked ribs as Jesus held her tenderly, though she could not hear his voice saying, "Daughter, you are made in my own image. You have not sinned by wanting to be yourself."

As the Greek woman hurried onto the windy beach, she saw a man sitting alone on a rock, and other men scattered along the beach.

She did not know which man was Jesus, whom she had heard performed amazing miracles—so many that some Jews said he was the Messiah himself. *My daughter must be healed,* she thought. *I cannot bear another day of seeing her pull her hair out, or of trying to wipe away the saliva dripping down her chin as she screams out horrible words. No child of God should live this way. There is no other option but that this man heal my daughter.*

She approached Peter, who stood with his fishing net, thinking. As she pulled her light brown cloak around her against the sea wind, she asked him, "Are you the one?"

Peter turned his head toward her, stared a moment before he registered who she was asking about, and then laughed loudly. "Not hardly. But thank you. Why would you think such a thing?"

"You look confident and solid, standing here so calmly," she said. "Where is he, if I may ask?"

"Jesus? Rabbi Jesus is over there," he pointed. "Yes, back there on that rock, the only one among us thirteen who is not looking curiously at you right now." Peter laughed again, and said, "I'm sorry I can't take you to him, but I'm responsible for supper. I don't know what Jesus will say to you, anyway. This is our vacation. How did you find us, anyway?"

The woman smiled briefly and said, "This man is my only hope." With that, she again wrapped her cloak around herself tightly and, heart pulsing, began the short walk to Jesus. As she came near him, she shouted above the sound of the waves, "Lord, son of David, have mercy on me! My daughter is demon-possessed and suffering terribly." Jesus had his eyes closed and she wondered if he had heard her. She again shouted, "Have mercy on me, son of David!"

When Jesus still did not respond, she turned back, running toward Peter and shouting, "Help me, you must help me speak to him!"

Peter was just casting out his net again. "I can't, like I said, I'm getting dinner. Um, maybe Andrew over there...."

The woman saw where he pointed and quickly called out, "Sir, help me, help me speak to Jesus. My daughter is tormented by a demon, and I must have Jesus' help."

Andrew replied, "Lady, if he won't talk to you, there's nothing I can do for you. I'm really sorry. But try John—he's coming back from a walk. See if he can help you."

She pulled her head covering back over her black hair, fearful that the men would think she was a prostitute. She ran to John, sand flying around her as she took each step. "You, sir, you know him well. My daughter is tormented by a demon. I need the Lord's help."

John's small but compassionate eyes rested gently on her worried face. "You must just ask him. He'll help you; I'm sure of it. But it's not good for you to be seen alone with all these men. Go to him quickly."

"No, no, you must come with me!" When John hesitated, she suspected it was because he didn't want to be seen alone with her, so she turned from him and shouted to Andrew, "Please come help me, you must!" And then she ran to Peter, "You, sir, please, my daughter must be more important than your fish. Help me, now!"

"Please, ma'am, we're not here for any reason but to rest," Peter said.

He glanced over at Simon and Judas, who were telling Jesus, "Send her away, for she keeps crying out after us."

Jesus looked over at the woman, who was now walking toward him slowly. She had begun to be afraid.

Her breath shortened as Jesus shouted over the sound of the waves and wind, "I was sent only to the lost sheep of the house of Israel." Once more, he focused on the sea.

She thought of giving up, but imagined her ten-year-old daughter, whose face contorted into expressions the woman had never seen in a human being. She thought, *If any one is lost, it is my little girl.* Falling before him on her knees in the wet sand, she said, "Lord, help me."

With sadness in his eyes and voice, yet still not looking at her, he replied, "It is not right to take the children's bread and toss it to the dogs."

Fiery anger raged in her heart and mind, burning away all confusion and leaving only determination. She remained kneeling before him, but these words snapped off her lips: "Yes it is, Lord. But even the dogs eat the crumbs that fall from their masters' table." Jesus looked down at her, eyebrows lifted. The woman held his gaze without blinking.

Then Jesus laughed. He laughed over and over again, like the waves washing over the shore. "Woman," he said warmly, "you have great faith! Your request is granted."

She closed her eyes and sighed. Though anger still simmered within her, relief and gratitude began to extinguish it. "Thank you, my Lord. You have saved our lives and I will never forget it." In seconds, she was running down the beach toward her home.

"Why did you change your mind, Jesus?" Judas put his hand on Jesus' shoulder, questioning.

"She is a true worshiper. She is truly a daughter of Abraham because she is a woman who believed God. She showed her faith through the very words that all of you wished would stop.

"Think about it, men. Which of you has ever won an argument with me?" Jesus laughed merrily again, looking down the beach as the woman disappeared into the trees.[1]

---

[1] A fictionalized version of Matthew 15:21-28.

Just what was Jesus doing?

In this Gospel passage, Jesus' actions provide an example of how a man might respond to an argument with a woman. Despite Jesus' initial silence and reluctance, he heard the woman's argument, conceded her point, praised her for her faith, and gave her what she asked.[2] He did not demand submission from "the Canaanite" woman, even though he was God's Son, and even though she was relatively powerless in this situation.

In contrast to how this story ends, many women experience arguments with men as both frightening and pointless. Those who have not experienced abuse may find it difficult to believe that Shau-Pei's situation still occurs, or they may believe it does not happen in industrialized society. Controlling relationships are very common, however. (For example, one in four women in the United States

---

[2] Jesus at first acted in what could be seen as an abusive manner toward "the Canaanite," however. He ignored her at first and then insulted her by referring to her people as "dogs" (Matthew 15:26). Jesus had certainly "called names" before when arguing with religious leaders (e.g., "whitewashed tombs," Matthew 23:27), but this woman was far from antagonistic toward him, as they had been. She had immense faith, as he credited her for, and was willing to do anything to bring about her daughter's deliverance. Scholars can only speculate as to what was going on here for Jesus, partly because there are still unknowns about Jewish culture in the Roman Empire. Jesus may have had assumptions about the woman because of her ethnicity. Perhaps he thought she would expect "magic" from him—expecting him to be like the magicians from her region—thinking at first she did not understand faith. Or maybe when he said "I was sent only to the lost sheep of Israel" (Matthew 15:24), he was simply referring to being in the first phase of his mission, which would eventually include Gentiles, but was focused only on Israel at that time.

reports having experienced an abusive relationship.[3]) But the abuse almost never happens in front of people outside the family. Hence, most people think it just doesn't happen anymore, or if it is happening to them, they may think they are alone.[4]

Controlling, intimidating behaviors are on a continuum. Sometimes the most deeply hurtful acts are the daily, drip-drip erosion that comes from insults, a cold shoulder, or other forms of disrespect. In many cultures around the world, a woman is expected to defer to the opinions of a man. While it is true that in North America, for example, a woman may speak her opinion, the question is, will she be heard? It's an unwritten rule that males generally have the authoritative voice. This too has an eroding effect on a woman's self-esteem.

It is not hard to imagine some of the reasons women stay in abusive relationships. The person who is the most important to you in the world treats you like dirt. Over time it would be easy to believe that you deserve it, especially when all your life you've heard and believed subtle and overt messages—from sources you trust, such as the church—about a woman's subordinate "place" in life.

Abusive Christian men, such as Man-Wei in this story, use Bible verses on submission to keep

---

[3] Patricia Tjaden and Nancy Thoennes, *Extent, Nature, and Consequences of Intimate Partner Violence* (Washington, DC: National Institute of Justice and the Centers for Disease Control and Prevention, 2000). Available on the Internet at http://www.ncjrs.gov/pdffiles1/nij/181867.pdf.

[4] If something about your relationship scares you, and you would like to talk to someone, call the National Domestic Violence Hotline: 1-800-799-7233 (SAFE).

control over their wives. Pastors, too often, tell abused women that wifely submission means accepting any kind of behavior from their husbands. Godly women may believe their pastors' egregious interpretation of Scripture and try to accept the abuse in order to be "good Christian" wives. Abusive men, even if they know something is "not quite right" about what they are doing, are reassured by their pastors that Scripture says it is their wife's duty to submit to them as they submit to God (a profound misreading of Ephesians 5:22; see Appendix B for more on submission).

Jesus, despite living in a culture with a hierarchical worldview, countered the grievous injustice of violence toward women by responding positively to a woman's sharp wit and faithful persistence, instead of intimidating her into accepting his decision as "final." As a Jewish rabbi, Jesus had no obligation to speak with this bold Gentile woman, particularly because she came to him unaccompanied (normally only "disreputable" women such as female slaves and prostitutes did such). Yet she is the only person recorded in Scripture to have won an argument with the Son of God, a rather high honor.[5] He did not make her submit to his point of view, but he gave her regard by listening to her and changing his mind. Jesus, the most secure male in history, was willing to submit to a woman. Reflect on that one!

---

[5] I first heard this statement in a New Testament class taught by Rikk Watts at Regent College. I have since been exposed to it in other feminist theological literature.

Questions for Reflection/Discussion

1. Compare the situations of Shau-Pei and the Gentile woman. How are they alike, and how are they different?

2. How are Man-Wei and Jesus different?

3. How does this Gospel story provide a corrective for distorted beliefs about the submission of women?

4. In many cultures in the world, women are expected to defer to the opinions of their husbands and other men. In North American and some other cultures, the expectation that women not be too outspoken can be more subtle and complex. In what circumstances has this cultural pressure affected you or someone you love?

5. Please read Appendix A on interpreting Scripture and Appendix B on submission, and then come back to these questions: What Scriptures are often distorted in order to keep women "in their place" with regard to their opinions and desires? What might be more accurate interpretation of these Scriptures, and why?

Meditation for Healing

Find a place where you can relax. Invite the Holy Spirit to come close and to help you be aware of being in Jesus' presence. (Even if you don't *feel* Jesus' presence, go ahead and affirm that presence.) Imagine arguing with Jesus about something you desperately want. Think of and/or write out a dialogue between the two of you, where you get the last word, then get what you long for, and where Jesus finally compliments you for your great faith. You are safe with Jesus.

And/Or: Recall a situation in which you felt stifled in being able to express your opinion because of your status as a woman. You kept silent because you did not feel safe, physically or emotionally. Perhaps you feared you would not be heard, or you would be judged because you are a woman. Imagine Jesus sitting next to you in the room, asking your opinion on the matter at hand. See yourself speaking out because Jesus asked you to do so. Note how he does not interrupt, and how he shows he is listening in the carefulness of his responses. He praises you for speaking out. He does not insult or hurt you in any way. Remember that Jesus, as the perfect representation of God, shows you how God listens and responds to your voice every day.

If you've heard that women and men shouldn't cominister...

chapter 8

I had always been more comfortable looking down at a calculator than leading a church group, but I still said yes to our pastor's request. Persuasion was his strength.

"Samantha," he said (everyone called me Sam, except him), "I think you're the person to co-lead the marriage ministry with Stuart." Then he noted how I plan ahead and am organized, and what a devoted wife and mother I am. He ended by saying that Stuart's wife did not feel she was the person to help him, for some reason.

I did have a good marriage, but I'd tended to take a literal "back seat" in the church most of my life. I took on some church fund-raising projects a couple of times, but I'd felt fulfilled using my leadership skills at work in my job as a certified public accountant. I should have remained content with that.

My meeting with Stu took place one Sunday afternoon at Dan's Donut Shop. When he'd called me on the phone about this meeting, he had a serious, businesslike tone in his voice. "Sam, I hear Pastor would like us to work together. We should meet and talk about this."

"Absolutely. I want to hear all about your plans and hopes for the ministry, and see what you think I can contribute," I had said. He didn't reply, but went on to discuss a date and time for us to meet.

At the appointed time, I purchased my donut and coffee and had my laptop open, ready to take notes on our meeting. Stu arrived ten minutes late and didn't bother to buy anything. He sat down, pulled in his chair, and said, "I wanted to tell you this directly, Sam, instead of through the pastor or on the phone. I just want you to understand it's nothing personal at all. I'll make it short: I don't do ministry with women. Too many men have fallen due to temptations from working closely with women in the ministry. It's not that that would happen with us, of course, but I just have a policy of never doing it. I'm sorry."

He stood up so quickly his chair almost turned over. Then he shook my hand and walked out.

I leaned back, trying to process what he'd said. I had been so out-of-touch with what goes on behind-the-scenes in churches that it never even occurred to me that people still operated in this manner. I was certainly fine with not being a part of the marriage ministry. After all, I had been asked, I had not volunteered. But I was not fine with Stuart's attitude toward women. The unspoken message was that women are dangerous to men who are committed to living sexually pure lives, as though Christian women are not also committed to do the same.

The next day I called our pastor and told him what happened.

He said, "I'm really sorry. Stuart sort of alluded to this but said he wanted to talk to you himself. I'll call him again and see if I can help him change his mind. I just wish there were some precedent for women and men working together in the Bible. I'm fine with it, of course, but it's hard to prove with Scripture that it's okay. All the disciples were men."

I looked at my husband who was watching me across the living room, and shook my head to communicate, "You won't believe what I'm hearing." Then I cleared my throat and said, "Huh. Interesting. I thought Jesus had some women followers too. Well, I'm fine with not doing this. Whatever works, Pastor." I don't think my tone hid the frustration and disgust I felt, but he didn't seem to pick up on it.

"Thanks so much for understanding, Samantha, and being willing to help out. I'll let you know if anything changes. We'll see you Sunday."

I hung up and sat staring at the phone. "So what if the disciples were all men? What in the world does that have to do with who leads the marriage ministry at our church?" I said, as though our pastor were still listening.

My husband answered instead, looking up from a book he was reading on quantum physics, "Good question. That whole 'only-men-were-disciples' thing seems to have been used a lot to keep women in the kitchen at church. Haven't you noticed?"

I *hadn't* noticed. I had thrown myself into my job, been very successful, well-respected by men and women alike, and had assumed that misogynist thinking in the church was a thing of the past.

I now had to return to the Bible. I knew the culture it was written in favored men. But I had to figure out just what was in there that kept people like Stu thinking this way about working with women, and that made my pastor unable to argue any differently. If there really wasn't precedent in the Bible for women and men ministering together, maybe I would have to rethink the whole Christianity thing. Maybe it wasn't for me, after all.

"Judas, do we have enough money to stay at this inn?" Peter asked. Everyone stopped at the door.

Joanna thought, We'd better. I just gave him what we need for a month's worth of travel and food.

But Judas's face and apologetic shrug revealed that he thought they had less than they needed. This happened frequently—the money never seeming to be quite enough. Tensions occurred on a daily basis between the men and the women providing for them, so Joanna chose not to pursue this issue with Judas now.

Instead she asked, "Don't we know someone we could stay with in this town?"

Jesus said, "Yes, we do. Susanna, what about your cousin? Remember we met her in the market the last time we came through here together?"

"I'd completely forgotten about that. I hardly know her, but I'm sure she'd help us," Susanna said. "Yes, I remember now. She lives in the middle of town. Her husband is a silversmith."

They wandered down the road together, watching the town darken in the twilight. Jesus said, "Tomorrow the ministry begins again. Early tomorrow, I'll be up to pray in the hills. Don't look for me. I'll come back when it's time to begin, and we'll spend some time talking to the Father together. Only he knows what he has planned for us. And, Joanna, don't worry about money. Our Father in heaven has provided bread for today, and for all the days past."

"Yes, Lord, you're right," Joanna said. Susanna and Mary nodded in agreement. They had such joy in being able to provide financially for everyone the past few months of Jesus' "kingdom-of-God" preaching tour. In Capernaum and other cities, they had seen the whiteness of leprosy turned to flesh; the crossed, glazed eyes of the blind come into focus; and the deaf hear their names for the first time. Because of all this, they had seen people believe that Jesus was the Messiah. Could Jesus not do another miracle of providing for them to the end? Susanna, Mary, and Joanna felt the glow of their shared, though unspoken, memories, and linked arms and walked ahead with all the other women.

James took Peter aside and they walked more slowly in order to speak confidentially. James whispered, "Only Jesus could make me agree to such an arrangement as this—traveling around with these women. And with them supporting us! This just goes against my grain."

Peter replied, quietly as well, "I know what you mean. Yesterday I had a run-in with a fellow—a man waiting in line at the bakery. He told me I should be ashamed of myself."

James said, "Jesus is a great man, but I admit I just don't understand him sometimes."

Jesus turned to the men from up ahead, and winked.[1]

---

[1] A fictionalized version of Luke 8:1-3.

Just what was Jesus doing?

Just as my elaboration of Luke 8:1-3 suggests, Jesus' choice to travel with women would have been seen as outrageous to outsiders as well as to his male disciples. Greek philosophers had women among their followers, but the average Jewish person would have had no respect for such a situation.[2]

The Talmud[3] warns men against talking "excessively" with women, as this could "lead you to adultery."[4] The remedy for keeping women from talking with men, and men from looking at women, was to keep women at home. One rabbi writes, interpreting Genesis 1:28: "The man subdues the woman so she will not go out into the marketplace, for the inevitable end of every woman who goes out into the marketplace is to fall into [sexual] sin."[5]

Apparently, Jesus did not believe these things about women. Instead, he confronted the culture's view of woman as "temptress." Jesus

---

[2] Another unusual aspect of this situation was the financial support the women provided for Jesus. Sometimes women served as "patrons," providing for an artist or philosopher, but it was uncommon for women to be in a financial position to do this, as Joanna, Susanna, and Mary (and "many others," according to Luke 8:3) apparently were.

[3] Rabbinic commentary on Scripture.

[4] Tal Ilan, *Jewish Women in Greco-Roman Palestine*, 126. (Talmud reference: bNed. 20a.)

[5] Tal Ilan, *Jewish Women in Greco-Roman Palestine*, 128. (Talmud reference: Gen. R. 8.12.)

was willing to risk a bad reputation to ensure that women were among his disciples, learning from him, participating in the ministry, and supporting him financially. Is this how God would act if God came down to earth? Apparently so! Women are made in God's image, just as much as men are—they are not more sinful than males, not more sexual than males, and not a snare to men's purity.[6] Jesus was willing to stake his good name on that.

As Samantha discovered in the opening story, some Christian men still hold that age-old male fear of woman as "seductress." Women as well may embrace a policy to not minister with men, as a form of godliness. (Coministry inevitably involves being alone together, as coministers must pray, plan, and even travel together if need be). Regardless of the motive, the effect of this "cultural law" is that women are kept on the sidelines of ministry, off to minister by themselves or with children and other women. Consequently, women not gifted in office work, children's ministry, or women's ministry have no place to offer their gifts. And so they take their gifts into other parts of the world where they are appreciated. This cultural belief regarding "woman as temptress" is reflected in rabbinic Judaism, but cannot be found in the New Testament.

---

[6] In fact, other stereotypes say just the opposite—that women are more virtuous than males, less sexual than males, and more spiritual than males.

According to Luke 8:1-3, Jesus did not have the fear of women (nor did he encourage women to have a fear of men) that sometimes prevails in churches now. He welcomed women into his ministry and leaned on their resources. Women were, in fact, disciples of Jesus. According to the definition of the time, Mary Magdalene, Joanna (the wife of Herod's steward Chuza), and Susanna were Jesus' disciples because they followed him and learned from him. Matthew included women as disciples (note what I have emphasized in the last sentence of this quotation): "Many women were also there, looking on from a distance; they had followed Jesus from Galilee and had provided for him. Among them were Mary Magdalene, and Mary the mother of James and Joseph, and the mother of the sons of Zebedee. When it was evening, there came a rich man from Arimathea, named Joseph, who was *also* a disciple of Jesus" (Matthew 27:55-57 NRSV). Matthew saw the women as disciples as much as he saw the rich man Joseph as a disciple. Moreover, disciples participated in the supernatural ministry of Jesus (such as the seventy in Luke 10).

Jesus wasn't the only person in the New Testament recorded as ministering with women. Believe it or not, Paul wrote about his ministry with women. Read Roman 16:1, where Phoebe is a minister in the church at Cenchrea and Paul's benefactor.[7] Read Romans 16:3, in which Paul lists Priscilla as a "coworker." In Acts 18:26, Priscilla is listed before her husband as a teacher of Apollos. She is again greeted before her husband in 2 Timothy (4:19), implying that Paul had asked her to tend to the Ephesian church, a hotbed of false teaching.[8] And, again in Romans 16:7, Paul lists Junia, a woman and relative of his, as "prominent among the apostles" and someone

---

[7] Bible translators often choose *deacon* or *servant* instead of *minister* for Phoebe. However, for the same Greek word (διακονοσ) they often choose *minister* for Tychicus in Ephesians 6:21, *minister* for Epaphras in Colossians 1:7, and *minister* again for Tychicus in Colossians 4:7. It seems some translators find it difficult to believe that a woman could be a minister in the early church, but readily apply that title to a man.

[8] It was uncommon for a woman's name to be listed before her husband's, just as it is now. This reverse ordering indicates Priscilla was the more prominent minister of the two. Note also, that 1 Timothy 2 is the passage often used to keep women from teaching or leading men. Timothy was in Ephesus when Paul wrote this. Second Timothy 4:19 makes it clear that Priscilla was also in Ephesus, serving at the church, likely in a teaching position given her history of teaching Apollos in Ephesus, as recorded in Acts 18.

who was imprisoned with him along with her husband or relative Andronicus.[9]

The pastor in the first story had much biblical precedent for attempting to change Stu's mind about ministering with women, if only he had known these things. They are here to see, but some scriptural facts will remain invisible when we Christians let culture—church culture, Hebrew culture, or Greco-Roman culture—and not Jesus' love dictate our moral standards.

---

[9] Usually, Junia is translated as a male name that did not exist in Paul's time. Why is it translated this way? We all have "lenses" through which we see Scripture. If translators believed that it was impossible for there to have been a woman apostle, they would not see what is really in the text—a woman apostle!

Questions for Reflection/Discussion:

1. What "cultural laws" did Jesus break in order to include women among his disciples in this passage from Luke 8?

2. Why do you suppose Jesus was not afraid to travel with, be seen with, and be financially supported by women?

3. What do you think is at the heart of the fear of men and women working together?

4. What would it look like for Christian men today to follow Jesus' law of love instead of giving in to the cultural—and very hurtful—view of woman as temptress?

Meditation for Healing

Have you ever felt you were not considered for a ministry position because a male coworker was afraid to work with women? If so, find a place where you can relax. Invite the Holy Spirit to come close and to help you be aware of being in Jesus' presence. (Even if you don't *feel* Jesus' presence, go ahead and affirm that presence.) Write or type out Luke 8:1-3, and add your own name in place of Mary Magdalene's, Joanna's, and Susanna's. Read over this "new" Scripture prayerfully. Ask Jesus to help you imagine yourself as a disciple of his, among the other women disciples. Picture some of the disciples as those in your life who have hurt you by overlooking you for coministry due to your gender. Ask Jesus to reveal to you what he would tell you in front of them. How would he affirm your calling to work with him—and with men?

If you don't have the emotional energy to "succeed" in ministry...

chapter 9

I'd rather pick up the phone than pick up the bottle, Dorothy thought as she dialed the telephone number of her AA sponsor, Monica. Alcoholics Anonymous had been a savior to Dorothy—not like Jesus was, but a close second. She had never experienced the kind of acceptance in church that she had in her AA meetings. But she had met Jesus in the church, and she knew going to church was the right thing to do. So she stayed—even though few people really understood her history and its impact on her current struggle to stay sober.

Dorothy had had her first taste of beer at the age of seven, during one of those very long days and nights when her mother was mysteriously and frighteningly absent. Dorothy had been looking for something to eat. In the refrigerator, she saw a cold, green "adult" bottle, with a pretty, red and gold label on it. Curiosity more than hunger told her to open the bottle. *Will this make me seem older? Will it make me angry, like Mom is when she comes home and wakes me up at four in the morning?* Dorothy spit the beer out into the sink that day. But there would be many lonely days in her growing-up years, and she got used to the taste of beer. Dorothy's mother never seemed to notice; she usually drank away from home despite keeping beer in the fridge for the occasional guest.

Now, Dorothy's own refrigerator held diet ginger ale and juice, and was full of food. She had been sober for three years. She attributed this to God, AA, and her sponsor…and her church. She always knew that she wanted to serve in the church, but had never felt worthy to do so until recently, after her third anniversary of sobriety.

When Monica finally picked up the phone, Dorothy said, "Monica, it's me. Got a minute?"

"Oh, yeah, sure, Dorothy. How are you?"

"I'm really sorry to be calling you again. I'm feeling like a failure right now," she laughed. "It's that prayer chain I was telling you about starting a few months ago. Do you remember?"

"Yes, you were pretty excited about it. What happened with it?"

"Well I did start it. I wanted to be faithful with it. It's my first real attempt at church ministry, you know? But it seems like it's already fallen apart. People aren't calling people. I know I should find replacements, but I just haven't. I can't seem to find the energy…" Dorothy absent-mindedly began looking in her kitchen cabinets for a bag of chips she knew was there.

Monica sighed. "Dorothy, look at you. Look how far you've come. I can't believe you're feeling so critical of yourself again. Do you really think other people are that critical?"

Dorothy raised her eyebrows as she opened the pantry door, wishing she could have such a trusting view of the world. "People really are that critical sometimes, Monica. Our pastor's wife told me she thought that if I was going to do something for God, I should try to do it right. I should follow through on my commitment. It really ticked me off, but I guess it's true. I don't know what's wrong with me. I just don't have enough energy or motivation or something." She sank down into an arm chair in the living room and began opening the bag of sour cream and chives potato chips.

The volume of Monica's voice began to rise. "It's no wonder, Dorothy. Don't you think God knows what you're up against? You're depressed, you're anxious, you're still fighting the urge to drink. What else?"

Dorothy quickly finished the list: "I've only been off cigarettes for a month and I need one right now; I have fibromyalgia, which makes it hard to want to move; the Prozac's not working for me; and my doctor is out of town on one of his vacations." She grimaced at the sound of her complaining voice, and sighed, "But I can't get off that easy. We all have excuses. I'm just lazy. I lie around here on my days off and watch the soaps. I'm sure God's not happy with *that*." She looked into the open bag of chips and wished she could get off the phone so she could just sit and eat.

"I'm just trying to get through your head that healing is a process. All you can do is give what you have today, even if it's so small that no one would even notice but Jesus."

"Mmm. Yeah. Well, I gotta go," Dorothy said, unconvinced and feeling even worse than before she had called.

"No, not that easy. One of these days you're gonna believe me when I say Jesus doesn't judge you like you judge yourself, or like others might judge you. I want you to read that passage we talked about last Sunday in Mark 12." Dorothy heard shuffling on the other line as Monica flipped through her Bible. Monica continued, "Yep, here it is…Mark 12…41-44. Read that and call me back and tell me what you think about how it applies to you."

"All right. I can do that," Dorothy replied, feeling a little lift. *At least I can say I read the Bible today if someone asks*, she thought, setting the bag of chips on the floor, and heading for her room where her Bible lay under a heap of clothes.

Rachel moved slowly through the court of women until she reached the temple-shaped coffer.

She had lost her husband two years earlier. He had been a Zealot and ten years older than her, so she had always known she would some day be alone. She had not counted on it happening so quickly, but her husband seemed to often be the first to volunteer for the next attack on the Romans. She was only twenty-eight years old. She was living with her mother, and two of her brothers and their families. She did have her own room, tucked into a wall surrounding their family's courtyard, but she did not have much else. She had her memories, but many of those were as unwanted as a lame donkey— or, as her husband would say, an evil wife. He had often jokingly quoted ben Sirach, the apocryphal Jewish writer, when he wanted her to be a little less outspoken: "A sandy ascent for the feet of the aged—such is a garrulous wife for a quiet husband." Of course, her husband was not exactly quiet, and she would always point this out to him.

Despite her freedom of speech with her provocative husband, Rachel was, in fact, a fair model of ben Sirach's esteemed silent, submissive wife—but only because she lacked the energy to be otherwise. She was often sad, having borne the fate of miscarriage after miscarriage. The one child who met the blessed light of day had died when he was two months old, of a very terrible cough. Her husband showed her kindness by not divorcing her, even though she was as good as barren.

When her husband died, Rachel grieved as well, but then one summer day she woke up when it was still cool, and realized things were going to get better. Her husband had no brothers, so she was in no danger of having to marry right away, according to levirate law. She was alone, and so there could be no more deaths for her, as long as she was able to avoid remarriage entirely. That would be her goal. She would devote her life to God now. All the love she had to give to children—and even perhaps a husband—this would go to the Lord and the Lord's temple.

So the widow Rachel brought to the temple all the money she had, two small coins. She now gladly tossed both into the coffer. She believed, as her husband had, that some day there would come a Messiah, and he would save them from the evil empire and even from the cruelty of life. She knew that the temple system was far from perfect. She and her husband had often discussed how Herod's gild on the magnificent building only emphasized how different this temple was from Solomon's. She trusted that God was larger than the temple, however, and would use even *her* gift toward the coming kingdom.

Jesus' recent militant act against the temple caused her wonderment. This morning he'd asked the crowd, "Why do the teachers of the law say that the Messiah is the son of David? David himself, speaking by the Holy Spirit, declared, 'The Lord said to my Lord, "Sit at my right hand until I put your enemies under your feet."' David himself calls him Lord. How then can he be his son?" Having said such a thing, could Jesus be the political savior she and her husband had awaited? If so, perhaps he wouldn't mind her tiny gift. This thought crossed her mind as the coins clinked as they landed in the treasury. She looked up, only to see Jesus sitting a few feet away, watching her. When her eyes caught his, his face lit up with a smile that would carry her through her darkest memories, in years to come.

Rachel quickly looked away, realizing she was in public, in a holy place, and he was a rabbi. But Jesus continued to look in her direction as he called the Twelve over. He said, loudly enough for her to hear: "Truly I tell you, this poor widow has put more into the treasury than all the others. They all gave out of their wealth; but she, out of her poverty, put in everything— all she had to live on."

She saw the men staring in her direction, the disbelief on their faces. She blushed and returned her gaze briefly toward Jesus, long enough to absorb the fact that someone great cared about her, and that he saw the love behind her little gift.[1]

---

[1] A fictionalized version of Mark 12:35-37, 41-44.

Just what was Jesus doing?

It isn't often that someone decides to give her last two pennies to a church, as this widow gave to the temple. But what is common is the effort that many women make to serve God and people, sometimes when they have few emotional resources from which to give. Depression strikes more women than men (by self-report, anyway—it's possible women are more willing to seek help for it than men are).[2] Women are also more likely to be sexually abused as children (again, by self-report), and so may have more emotional hurdles in their paths as adults.[3]

Women are also most likely to be a part of and serve in the church—to give of their time, their hearts and minds, their resources. (Usually, about 60 percent of church members are women.[4]) Women serve by nurturing babies and toddlers in the nursery; by teaching Sunday school to children and other women; by coordinating prayer; by planning social events; by taking care of administrative work in the office; by leading worship; by giving financially; and they even sometimes serve as deacons, elders, teachers, pastors, and preachers. Jesus knows what each woman has to give, and judges each accordingly. Some women have enjoyed childhoods in which they were respected and loved by two parents with a stable marriage. Others have suffered abuse, grief, or pain and need time, love, prayer, and therapy to recover, even as they give from their hearts to serve the church. Jesus understands each person's obstacles to growth and ministry, and did not and does not judge like his followers might.

---

[2] See Agneta H. Fischer, ed., *Gender and Emotion: Social Psychological Perspectives*, to address the complexities of the potential reasons for gender differences in emotional expression, including depression. See also the National Institute of Mental Health's web page: http://www.nimh.nih.gov/publicat/depwomenknows.cfm#sup1.

[3] See the American Psychological Association's web page: http://www.apa.org/releases/sexabuse/victims.html.

[4] Cynthia Woolever and Deborah Bruce, *A Field Guide to U.S. Congregations: Who's Going Where and Why* (Louisville, KY: Westminster John Knox Press, 2002).

Jesus displayed this different kind of standard in the example of the widow giving her "last two cents," so to speak. Given the value of status in Jesus' culture, it is surprising that he chose a lowly widow and a "mere" woman as a model of spirituality. In New Testament times, widows and orphans were the most vulnerable members of society. They were likely to be poor due to their loss of economic support from the husband and father. Moreover, in Judaism, few women were spiritual leaders, and almost no women bore the title of "rabbi." Women (and slaves) were exempted from many of the religious requirements that men had to fulfill.

Jesus pointed to the widow's poverty and lack of spiritual and economic status to highlight the hypocrisy of religious leaders who tried to impress others with their largess, yet treated the widows like this one unjustly (Mark 12:35-40). The woman is an example of the kind of religion Jesus respected—the kind that draws a person to put in all she has (Mark 12:44) yet not for others to see. Such generosity of spirit happens all the time—every day and every week in churches all over the world, from women who have very little to give, whether physically or emotionally. Just as it didn't matter to Jesus that the woman's paltry amount of money was only going to a wasteful temple system, neither does it matter if what you do for God does not appear successful to others. Jesus receives the gift with arms open wide, because he sees your heart.

Questions for Reflection/Discussion

1. What are some of the "cultural laws" in our society and churches that make both Dorothy and "the widow" surprising role models?

2. Does Dorothy remind you of someone you know? Have you made judgments about this woman? Is the woman ever *you*? Explain your responses.

3. You may tend to love and accept women like Dorothy, who struggle emotionally and/or with addictions. But what do you tend to judge harshly in others and in yourself? Why do you think you do this?

4. What can you tell from the Gospel passages presented here about how Jesus judges us? How do his standards surprise you?

Meditation for Healing

Find a place where you can relax. Invite the Holy Spirit to come close and to help you be aware of being in Jesus' presence. (Even if you don't *feel* Jesus' presence, go ahead and affirm that presence.) Imagine (or write about, or draw) yourself entering heaven and finding yourself in a large room with a great crowd of friends and strangers. You realize that each life is being reviewed. Jesus approaches you and places a gold crown on your head, one with multicolored precious gems. He speaks of all the obstacles you had to overcome, even to return his love, and he praises you in front of all. The reproach you fear never comes. You feel his love, approval, and complete acceptance, and the eyes of all the people in the crowd reflect back these same feelings toward you.

If you've been encouraged to deify motherhood...

chapter 10

Last week, I was graced with a rare occurrence—all three of my children were asleep at the same time! I stood for a moment, gazing at the faces of my open-mouthed (drooling!), long-lashed, sleeping children—my ever-nursing little six-month-old, my two-and-a-half-year-old whose middle name is "No," and my industrious four-year-old. Then I turned and took a step right into a clump of Play-Doh. Smiling, I peeled it off my foot. I stepped over all the creaky boards in the room and closed the door without a click. I was free! I finally had some time to myself...but I had no idea how to spend it.

It used to be so easy to know what to do with spare time. Even if my husband was off doing something else (he loves to golf), I could jump into my gray and purple hiking boots and drive out to the mountains for a hike. I love creation—just being in the middle of it in all its stillness yet unpredictability. I would take my little New Testament; a notebook to write down my inspired thoughts; and my favorite picnic lunch of cheese, rye bread, and fruit. But, those days of hopping in the car are over. Getting in the car can take half a day with three little children!

So I considered finishing an article by James Dobson I'd started reading two days earlier. Then it occurred to me that I could even take a bath—with those lavender bath salts I'd received for my birthday more than a year ago. But then I told myself I should read the Bible. I didn't really have time with God anymore. I prayed in the shower—my two-minute, every-other-day "me-time" shower.

It had taken me a long time to figure out how to spend time with God, how to pray. In my late teens, I finally developed an easy relationship with God. Before then I'd always struggled with how to "do" times with God. I'd had a breakthrough when, at a women's retreat in the mountains, I realized that I could use my love for the outdoors and for writing to connect with God. I learned to write my prayers, outdoors, even if that meant just sitting on the front porch as the sun was setting. I liked praying for people I knew at work and in my neighborhood.

I'm so different now. My concerns revolve around making workable menus for finicky little stomachs, having garage sales with toys and kids' clothes, and arranging play dates. And it's not like I'm this perfect mother either. Sometimes I just want to run away—or at least take a long vacation in the Bahamas.

I knew I needed to try to return to having times with God. So I got out my old, coverless Bible. But then all the old confusions about how to "do quiet time" came back to me, and I just left it on the table and chopped veggies for dinner, instead.

Then on Sunday, just after the service was over, I spotted Beth, and realized she might be able to help me. I walked up to her as she was leaving her pew, and said, "Hi, Beth. I need to talk to you about something. I'm wondering if you have a few minutes." When she said, "Of course!" we moved back into the pew and sat down.

I continued, "I just need someone to talk to about my spiritual life and you seem like the perfect person. You've raised seven children! I really can't imagine how you did it and stayed such a good Christian. Sometimes I feel like I'm going crazy, like I've lost myself and my faith too. There's no time for prayer or Bible reading or anything spiritual at all."

Her response really surprised me, despite the fact that everything she said seemed familiar. She took my hand, looked me in the eye and said, "You know, hon, I have found one thing to be true. There really is no higher calling than motherhood." She said I was being spiritual by being a mother, and that God would reward me. And then she said, "But a really good babysitter might help you out there too. Every woman needs some time to herself."

Just then my two preschoolers ran down the aisle, waving Popsicle-stick art and yelling "Mommy,

Mommy!" I laughed. She had no idea how *much* I needed time to myself! We did have a good sitter, but could only afford her once a week for our "date night."

"Sweetie," Beth said. "This time passes so quickly. Stay true to your calling. Mothering is what women were created to do." She patted me on the shoulder as she stood to leave.

It sounded good, though it left me feeling uneasy. But I trusted her opinion—seven kids! So later that day I put my Bible on the shelf with all the other books I will probably never read until middle age. I felt a weight of guilt lift off my shoulders, but a sadness settle down in its place. *Is this really all my spiritual life's about now?* I thought. *Diapers, sand boxes, and Play-Doh?* I sighed and went downstairs to make dinner.

The day that Jesus rebuked the woman in the crowd, the men had still been thinking about what had happened a few days earlier at Martha and Mary's home in Bethany.

The two sisters—former slaves who had never married and who shared a thriving business making wedding clothes[1]—had opened their home to Jesus and his twelve disciples. The disciples couldn't get over what a cook Martha was. And the food never stopped coming! They loved her spicy lentil soup, her barley bread, and especially her fish. (They didn't always eat very well on the road.) But Mary amazed the men in a different way. She asked Jesus to teach her about God. Mary and Martha could read and write and had learned some of the Torah. Their brother, a self-educated man and a former slave himself, had taught them. But almost never did a woman attempt to follow a rabbi, as that meant she wanted to be a teacher herself!

But apparently that's what Mary wanted, because she sat at Jesus' feet, as the male disciples often did, while her sister served every meal. Jesus not only tolerated this outrageous behavior, he also defended Mary

---

[1] No one knows the true marital status of Mary, Martha, and Lazarus. Being unmarried, however, was very unusual in that society. Even widows usually quickly remarried due to the severe economic consequences of not doing so. But emancipated slave women would often be overlooked for marriage because of their former "loose" history—maidservants were often used sexually and were seen as nothing more than prostitutes. It is possible that Mary, Martha, and Lazarus were all former slaves with their father's identity unknown or their father simply rejecting them entirely because he was married (to someone not their mother) with children.

» motherhood is good, but not divine «

when Martha pointed out her sister's lack of helpfulness. "Martha, Martha," he said, "you are worried and upset about many things; but few things are needed—or indeed only one. Mary has chosen what is better, and it will not be taken away from her."

The men had never seen such a thing, and secretly felt that something was amiss in Jesus' attitude. Really, Mary should have been helping Martha cook, clean, and serve. It was the women's role to provide hospitality.

After this curious behavior on Jesus' part, Jesus insisted that he and the men stay at the women's home for a few days. Thinking this would certainly provoke a feud between the sisters, several of the men quietly talked to each other about wishing they could move on. They also did not like how it looked—all these men staying in the home of two women, former slaves at that, with their brother off at work most of the time.

Their discomfort continued. The next day the twelve men and the two sisters joined a large crowd that formed when word got out that Jesus was a prophet with special power. Most of the people thrilled when Jesus commanded a demon to leave a man who was unable to speak and the man then spoke. Some of them could not believe such a thing could happen by God's power; they accused Jesus of using demonic power. Jesus explained patiently how Satan's kingdom could not stand if Satan cast out demons, and pointedly asked his accusers how their own exorcists managed to remove the demons. He then warned them about the vulnerable state of one who has had demons cast out; if the exorcists do not understand the kingdom of God, those whom they "help" will be in trouble.

At that point the atmosphere became rife with a sense of foreboding, even doom. When Jesus said, "Whoever is not with me is against me, and whoever does not gather with me scatters," it was clear he was asking them to make a choice: Will you stand with me, or will you stand on the side of evil?

Then, as the tension grew unbearable, a woman's voice burst forth from the crowd: "Blessed is the mother who gave you birth and nursed you!" This was a common saying when one wanted to praise someone. Jesus rejected the woman's praise, however, as a distraction. Instead he praised the woman by saying that she, too, had to make a choice about Jesus: "Blessed rather are those who hear the word of God and obey it!"

John cringed. It's one thing to publicly rebuke other important religious men—well, that was bad enough—but for Jesus to publicly correct a "mere" woman who was only praising him? On the way back to Martha's house, John murmured an apology to the women. Mary said, "No. Jesus was simply telling us our worth. Women, too, should listen to and obey God's word."

Martha nodded, and added, "Mary, you'd better start listening to God about what to do about dinner!"

They laughed and continued on their way.[2]

---

[2] A fictionalized version of Luke 10:38-42; 11:14-28.

» *motherhood is good, but not divine* «

Just what was Jesus doing?

Having children changes life, whether you as "Mommy" are the primary caregiver, or whether you and your husband are raising the children together more or less equally. It can seem that even though your life has been enriched by the beauty and joy your baby brings, it has also been reduced to diaper wipes and teethers. When you hear at church that "motherhood is a woman's highest calling," you can begin to feel that it's true—because there is truly no time to grow spiritually in the ways that you did before you gave birth to a child.

In Jesus' culture, bearing and raising children—especially male children—was a woman's highest purpose in life. The main purpose of marriage itself was producing offspring. In fact, rabbinic law said that a man should divorce his wife if, after ten years of marriage, she remained barren.[3] So the notion that motherhood is a woman's highest calling—a notion that is popular in some churches today—potentially comes from rabbinic Judaism.

But Jesus had a different perspective, for when a woman in the crowd called out a traditional blessing—"Blessed is the mother who gave you birth and nursed you!"—he corrected her, saying, "Blessed rather are those who hear the word of God and obey it." Jesus beckoned to an even higher calling for all mothers and women.

---

[3] Tal Ilan. *Jewish Women in Greco-Roman Palestine*, 112. (Talmud reference: mYeb. 6.6.)

This passage underscores the story about Mary and Martha. In that story Jesus also affirms the spirituality of women. The saying "motherhood is a woman's highest calling" implies that a woman need not bother herself with spiritual things—not to the degree that a man might—but should focus instead on marriage and children. Yet Jesus treated Mary and Martha (though they were likely single and may have been childless) not as women who missed their true callings in life, but as persons with great spiritual capacity.

Women did not often follow rabbis, as it was not considered appropriate for a woman to learn the Torah. Learning from a rabbi indicated a desire to teach the Law like a rabbi, which women were almost never allowed to do. Yet Jesus affirmed Mary's choice to shun her role as hostess in favor of sitting at his feet in the position of a disciple. One who "sat at the feet" of a great teacher aspired to be just like him (see Luke's report of Paul sitting at the feet of Rabbi Gamaliel in Acts 22:3).

Jesus' strong approval of Mary's desire to learn from him, as well as his seeming rebuke of the woman in the crowd, affirmed the way he saw women. Jesus did not see them as "baby makers" (although he welcomed mothers and children—see Luke 11). He did not even see them as having a primary calling to model faithfulness for their children. Rather, Jesus saw women as his own people, whom he longed to speak to and lead—"He gently leads those that have young" (Isaiah 40:11).

Questions for Reflection/Discussion

1. What do you predict for the spiritual life of the mom in the first story?

2. How was Jesus' correction of "the woman in the crowd" actually a sign of respect?

3. The things Martha did for Jesus were needed and appreciated, as are the things mothers do for their children. How can we avoid making "enemies" of Martha and Mary, or of motherhood and of listening obedience to Jesus? (If you're stumped on this one, try Brother Lawrence's book *Practicing the Presence of God*).

4. What "cultural laws" in our families, society, and churches can make it hard for mothers to seek out the highest calling of listening to and obeying Jesus?

Meditation for Healing

Perhaps you feel disappointed in your ability to be both a good mother and a good Christian. Maybe you feel it is an impossible task. The truth is, being a good mother *is* Christian service. But those who serve in any capacity can attest that burnout is the result of not tending to one's spiritual (as well as physical) needs. Try these on-the-run meditations to remind you that you are not just a womb, nor nursing breasts, and that your importance is not based on the outcome of your children's lives:

1. While watching your children play during a quieter period of the day, ask Jesus to show you what he saw in children when he said, "Truly I tell you, anyone who will not receive the kingdom of God like a little child will never enter it" (Luke 18:17). Ask him to give you that quality in greater measure.

2. Choose a short phrase (either from Scripture, from your own inner dialogue with God, or from some other meaningful source) to say to yourself over and over again while you are busy doing routine jobs. Examples include:

- God is our refuge and strength, an ever-present help in trouble. (Psalm 46:1)
- All shall be well, all shall be well, and all manner of things shall be well. (Juliana of Norwich)
- My soul glorifies the Lord, and my spirit rejoices in God my Savior. (Mary's prayer, Luke 1:46-47)
- Praise the Lord, my soul; all my inmost being, praise his holy name. (Psalm 103:1)

If you've ever felt your kids aren't welcome...

chapter 11

Viola relished the weeklong summer revival meetings at her church. The spastic colon condition Sister Trina had had for ten years might just be healed this time. Or even Brother Cecil's debilitating arthritis. It happened sometimes, and it could be that *your* prayers would be answered this time. The warm summer nights sparkled with energy, hope, and joy. There was comfort food—like fried chicken and potato salad—for the ones who were "give out," as they say in the South. But, of course, after five hours of a church service, that would be nearly everyone.

Viola remembered hating revival week as a child, because she would spend hours in her too-tight, black patent leather shoes. On top of that, she had to keep a huge bow on her head the entire time. But now, at twenty-three, with a child of her own, she could wear whatever she wanted (jeans and a T-shirt!). More importantly, she had reached a place in her faith where she loved to worship God, and yes, loudly and expressively.

She managed to get a precious nugget of truth from every preacher who came through.

The one thing that bothered her was leaving her three-year-old in the children's program for so long. She kept Joline with her for at least part of the time. But whenever she and Joline sat by parents who could afford babysitters and had left their children at home, Viola felt uncomfortable.

Like last night. Viola sat next to Brother Joe and Sister Celia. Viola was worshiping away, hands lifted, belting out praise to God. She had forgotten that Joline might get bored with coloring. Viola looked down and her daughter had Sister Celia's pink Bible. As the song came to an end, everyone could hear Joline's tiny voice comically break the holy silence: "Sister Celia, I want a pink Bible too!" Several people laughed and Viola smiled too.

Sister Celia had been deep in prayer and opened her eyes after a few moments. She stared coolly at Viola, and then she closed her eyes again. Viola felt a burning heat go through her, and it wasn't the Holy Spirit. She picked up her daughter and exchanged places with her so that she was no longer sitting next to Sister Celia, and then rummaged in her bag for some Oreos. She wasn't sure exactly why she was embarrassed, and angry at Sister Celia. She could understand the annoyance. But she felt like she always had to be on guard for what her little girl might say or do that would disturb the worshipers around her. The entire service was geared to adults. It was impossible for a child to enter in like everyone else. So even though her daughter had already been in daycare all day, Viola often felt compelled to leave Joline in the nursery or in the somewhat chaotic children's program.

Deep down Viola believed her daughter should be included in the worship service. Joline loved to worship God, just as much as the adults did. She danced and sang to her children's praise CDs at home. She knew all the stories about Jesus, and she knew he loved her. Just yesterday, she played "church service" with her Barbies. Malibu Barbie, overcome with the Holy Spirit, lay on the ground, worshiping God.

Viola stood up again as the worship continued—"Oh, victory in Jesus, my Savior forever"—but her heart wasn't in it anymore. She sang the well-worn song and kept an eye on her little girl, making sure she was busy. Before the preacher got up to speak, Viola gathered up Joline's toys, took her child's hand, and went home.

"Women and children!" a man exclaimed, as I entered the courtyard. Other men were just sitting down on the stone benches in Asher's courtyard.

I felt a little intimidated by this strange greeting, but the precious baby in my arms squirmed and whimpered. I lost my fear of the men, although my fear of my little girl's illness resettled deep in my stomach. My tiny baby, Mary, had diarrhea and was losing weight.

The women with me were my neighbors. We had decided that this Jesus, whom some swore must be the Messiah, should—and would—say blessings over our children. We'd heard about what he'd done in Capernaum; someone had an aunt and uncle from there who'd visited. Jesus had taken a child in his arms and said, "Whoever welcomes one of these little children in my name welcomes me; and whoever welcomes me does not welcome me but the one who sent me."[1] So, we found him at the Pharisee Asher's house. Asher had no choice but to let us in, as we weren't leaving. But we hadn't taken into account Jesus' followers.

"Swarms of women and children!" one of the men grumbled.

The men scowled and exchanged sour words for several minutes. Despite their unattractiveness, I decided to stand behind them, thinking that Jesus would appear

---

[1] Mark 9:36-37.

among them any moment. It turned out they were carrying on a most interesting conversation. Apparently, they felt irritable over what Jesus had said about divorce earlier that day. A few of them had left their wives and remarried other women, and they said Jesus had called them *adulterers*! All of them admitted to having contemplated divorce at one time or another. Currently, several of them had wives who complained about how often the men were gone, following after this Rabbi Jesus, who might or might not *really* be the Messiah. Jesus' teaching tethered them to the demands of their families, even though it was he who had called them to follow him in the first place. They complained, *Moses would never say such a thing! What rabbi would place his followers in such an impossible position!*

Clearly, these men were in a bad mood. I thought I was hidden from them, but suddenly one came up to me from the side and addressed me. "What are you doing here?"

I blushed and looked away.

"We're here for the children's sake, sir!" replied another woman standing nearby. She held her sleeping baby who suffered from a rash all over her body. "We would like Rabbi Jesus to bless the children."

The courtyard was full of "ssshhh" sounds, to little avail. Babies' cries, toddlers' whines, children's laughter and teasing made it difficult to hear adult voices. The woman spoke loudly enough to be heard in the rooms of the house, however. I knew that, like me, she was not going anywhere until she had what she wanted.

The men did not know what we knew about Jesus, I guess. They didn't know that he welcomed children. "The rabbi doesn't have time for you!" a bald man yelled out to us. "Go away!"

The children momentarily stopped their stirrings at such harsh words. But Jesus—I just knew it was him—suddenly stood up from where he had been conversing with two five-year-olds, the twin children of my best friend.

"Don't have time for them, Peter? That isn't true! Let the little children come to me, and do not hinder them, for the kingdom of God belongs to such as these. Truly I tell you," and it seemed he slowed his words down so they could hear the warning in his voice, "anyone who will not receive the kingdom of God like a little child will never enter it."

The men looked down, clearly humiliated. The Pharisee Asher, at Jesus' side, smiled knowingly as though he himself had loved and accepted children all along.

The man Jesus called Peter muttered to another of them, "We can forget the new Israel now."

Jesus did not seem to care about the men's feelings. He shooed them off the stone benches. I was the first to sit down with my sweet Mary, and other women with babies and toddlers followed. Three children tugged on Jesus' cloak at the same time. He laid his hands on their heads and recited blessings, giving thanks to the Creator for children. The woman with the loud voice carried her rash-covered baby to Jesus, and Jesus immediately stood up—as though the woman herself had authority—to put his hands on the baby!

I knew then we were safe. Despite the cool reception we received from Jesus' followers, Mary would be healed this day! We were welcomed, after all.[2]

---

[2] A fictionalized version of Mark 10:13-16.

Just what was Jesus doing?

Until I became a mother, I did not understand how it might feel to be separated from my infant or toddler in church. I never realized that if I kept my little one with me in the worship service, I might have judging eyes around me, expecting me to keep my child quiet or in the nursery. I learned quickly that neither North American society nor church culture really welcomes children. Their noise, their mess, their unpredictability, the fact that they require continual sacrifice on the part of parents and other adults—none of that meshes well with the things adults in our culture value, such as the ability to do what we want when we want and to see our goals accomplished, including the goal of a successful worship service.

Mothers and fathers adjust to our culture's expectations and even sometimes accept the line of thinking that infants, toddlers, and school-aged children are better off separated from the adults in church. Jesus, however, had a different attitude toward children—one that was just as countercultural then as it is today. He identified with them to such a degree that he said, "Whoever welcomes one of these little children in my name welcomes me" (Mark 9:37), and "The kingdom of God belongs to such as these" (Mark 10:14).

Children, however, were the weakest and most defenseless members of society in Jesus' time, subject to all kinds of illnesses that frequently resulted in death. When Jesus lifted up a child as a model of great spirituality (Mark 10:14), and insisted that the disciples learn how to enter the kingdom by being like a child (Mark 10:15), they probably did not understand him. While Jewish people did have a respect for humility—a respect that the Greeks did not possess during Jesus' day—the disciples probably expected the Messiah to exhibit political power. They were still thinking about Jesus' "greatness," and, hence, their own (see their argument in Mark 9:33-37). Their stern rebuke of the women and children followed; they had no time for the lowly in status and assumed Jesus viewed the women and children that way too.

That Rabbi Jesus took time to bless the children was unusual, and so was his implicit valuing of their mothers, the children's primary caretakers in that culture. The adults who came to Jesus with the children were most likely mothers and wet nurses, and female slaves accompanying them. Women. Women through the ages have valued children and identified with their own children in the same way Jesus does ("Whoever welcomes one of these little children in my name welcomes me," Mark 9:37). If someone shows our child love and respect, it often feels the same as showing *us* love and respect. By welcoming the children, Jesus gave these women regard, in contrast to the other men who rejected the women by rejecting their children.

Jesus demonstrated values that were very different from those of many of his followers. He welcomed children—with all their noise, needs, and kingdomlike unpredictability—into his church.

Questions for Reflection/Discussion

1. If you are a mother, what are some ways that you identify with Viola? Or even with Sister Celia? Whether or not you are a mother, have you ever wished that children were more valued or included in adult church services?

2. What cultural values in our society and churches conflict with the welcoming of children?

3. What struck you about Jesus in the Gospel story? What might Jesus (who is "the image of God," 2 Corinthians 4:4) reveal to you about who God is?

4. If Jesus were incarnated in your time and culture, what might a church service Jesus was leading look like? Where would the children be?

Meditation for Healing

Find a place where you can relax. Invite the Holy Spirit to come close and to help you be aware of being in Jesus' presence. (Even if you don't *feel* Jesus' presence, go ahead and affirm that presence.) Imagine (or write about, or draw) Jesus spending time with your child(ren) during an adult worship service. What would that be like? How would that experience be different or healing for both you and your child(ren)?

If you've felt left alone in your grief and pain...

chapter 12

Betsy Mae had the habit of talking to her bird. Today she said, "Keetie, these Meals-on-Wheels dinners are good, but nothing tastes good when you're alone."

The parakeet cocked its head.

Betsy Mae took this as a sign to go on. While tearing off a piece of whole wheat bun and pushing it through the bars of the bird's cage, she said, "I raised Jerry as best I could. When his dad died, I had to be a mother *and* a father to Jerry. A person can't do that very well—not really. He just went away from me. I took him to Sunday school every Sunday from before he could put a solid sentence together, and then he just stopped going one day. I couldn't talk sense into him. It's like he just couldn't hear a word I said anymore. He was so, so sad.

"But he wasn't bad, Keetie. No, he wasn't." Betsy Mae slowly carried the Styrofoam container of Thanksgiving turkey and gravy, green beans, and cranberry sauce to the refrigerator. Then she inched back to her well-worn armchair and sighed down into it. She began thumbing through her photo albums, as she often did since Jerry had gone to prison. Her photographs were her link to a life when she had been truly happy. They reminded her of who she was in her heart: not a widow on disability, not lonely, not heartbroken over her son, but free from aches and pains and, most certainly, free of gray hair.

Her photos told her the truth of her life. She lingered over a photo of Jerry as a newborn. She treasured it most of all. When he was born she and Gene had felt as though God had shown up at their front door. And there was the one picture of the three of them, taken at a Sears or Penney's portrait studio some twenty years ago, just months before Gene died. She'd talked them into getting their portrait done, as they hadn't had one made in years, and it so happened they'd all had haircuts that week. They'd made a day of it, going out to Shoney's for hot fudge cake afterward. They were happy that day, just being together—laughing, joking, teasing in all the old familiar ways. It showed in the picture—they were tickled at something, long forgotten now, but the joy of being family shone in their smiles. Not that they were happy every day, but whose family is always happy?

Gene never would have predicted that Jerry's life would take this path, she thought. "And neither would I," she said aloud. She wasn't very happy with the Lord right now. She turned to look at Keetie over by the door and said,

"Couldn't God have done something to prevent all this? Is there something I did to deserve this?" Then, she thought, chiding herself: *It's not like life is so horrible right now. I have this subsidized apartment, and I have friends here even though I can't get out to church much anymore. But my only son doesn't even believe. He didn't do what the police say he did, and he blames God that he's in jail. And I can't get out to visit him more than once in a while. He's alone on Thanksgiving. Mad at God—too mad to be grateful for anything—and I think he's mad at me too. And still mad at his dad for dying.*

Then she said aloud, "I've been praying for Jerry for ten years, and nothing. No real changes. You'd think God didn't know what it was like to have an only son taken away. But he does. He doesn't know what it's like to be me, though. Can't know what it's like to be a widow without her only son. Can't, or he'd get busy."

The little bird looked at her and chirped.

"If you've got something to say, Keetie, go ahead and say it. Don't hold back," Betsy Mae laughed. With her spirits lifted for a moment, she decided to say one more prayer for her son on this holiday. *Oh Lord, please, just please, give some comfort to Jerry this day. Show him one thing to be grateful for today. And help me believe that you know what I'm going through. That you really do care and haven't left me alone. Amen.*

*"Ever heard of Nain, Thomas?"
Peter whispered.*

"No. I think we're on a 'detour.'"

They were walking with Jesus and many other people with whom they were barely acquainted—men and women who had decided to follow Jesus for a time. It didn't seem to bother Jesus when people chose him instead of the other way around. But the Twelve were continually making adjustments to this, as they prided themselves on having been hand-selected by Jesus.

They were also reeling from Jesus' most recent healing—a Roman centurion's slave. Jesus was saying things lately that made it clear this kind of thing would keep happening. "Love your enemies, do good to those who hate you, bless those who curse you, pray for those who mistreat you"[1] and "Do not judge and you will not be judged"[2] and then the final blow, "Why do you call me 'Lord, Lord,' and do not do what I say?"[3] The men knew they had a lot to learn from Jesus, but they weren't sure this kind of teaching was really what they had signed up for. And here they were headed toward some hole-in-the-wall called Nain.

Jesus led the group of people and donkeys, since few knew where they were going. They saw the open city gate, up ahead, and all were glad at the thought of refreshment. Moments passed before the group spotted a

---

[1] Luke 6:27-28.

[2] Luke 6:37.

[3] Luke 6:46.

woman coming toward them through the entry. After her, it seemed the whole town poured out of the opening. Jesus' followers understood what was going on when they saw the dead man carried on the bier and heard the music—the too-familiar refrains filling them with sadness.

Jesus saw the dead man's mother crying alone, without a husband or other family to comfort her. He thought of the way Mary, his own mother, loved him, and he knew she would experience the same tearing away, suffocating, deep-in-the gut loss when the Romans and religious leaders finally did away with him. He remembered the many times, already, that he had felt similar grief over Jerusalem, which he thought of as his daughter. The Pharisees, Sadducees, and scribes had already refused to recognize him as the one sent to bring them peace. He saw Israel walking toward its own destruction, and knew in his heart his people would not receive salvation from him. This thought could bring Jesus to tears in a moment, because of his love—no, passion—for the people of Jerusalem. He felt like a mother hen who aimed only to gather her chicks under her wings and protect them.

The woman, too, had tried everything she could to protect her only child from suffering and death. Leaving the city gate reminded her of the times she, her son, and his friends had endured long trips to help him dip his legs into a healing pool. Neither water nor angels could wash away the disease in his body, and the doctors' fees soon far exceeded her resources. Sometimes she wondered, *Is God ignoring me because I do not worship at the temple in Jerusalem?*

She did not see Jesus approach her until he was very close. When he spoke to her those unbelievably tender words, "Don't cry," she wondered if he was an angel. She stopped crying, only because of the immense comfort given to her from this rabbi's compassion, and watched as Jesus walked up to the bier. She did not know what to expect. No one did. When he reached out and touched it, the bearers stood still.

Many of Jesus' disciples were shocked and inwardly reproachful—why would Jesus make himself unclean, for no reason? Did he not believe the man to be dead? Was it not too late to heal him?

Jesus looked down at the dead man and said, "Young man, I say to you, get up!" The corpse struggled to sit up. The bearers, hearts pounding wildly, nearly dropped the bier. Jesus unwrapped the man's head, and the man spoke one word, "Mother!" Jesus helped him off the bier and turned to his mother, who let out a shriek of unfettered joy.

What a torturous parting it had been this morning, when her son had slipped away from her forever. Now he had returned to her with the word *mother* on his lips, like a baby. Jesus' eyes filled with tears at the sight of this amazing rebirth. *Might Jerusalem one day be reborn as well?* he couldn't help thinking.

Fear seized the people of Nain. Death, they understood, but life after death? Only in the stories of the prophets did such a miracle occur. *Could it be Elijah returned?* some speculated. *With only a touch—not needing to place his whole body over the young man as Elijah had—he raises a widow's son.* "A great prophet has appeared among us!" many finally conjectured. Others began to exchange this sentence as though it were a greeting: "God has come to help his people!"

Thomas whispered to Peter, "I guess we'll be hosted well in *this* town tonight!"[4]

---

[4] A fictionalized version of Luke 7:11-17.

Just what was Jesus doing?

Life without the comfort of family—because of the death of a spouse or other family member, or a lifetime of unwanted singleness—can be miserable. Physical disability brings about further pain and isolation. If church has provided a family in the past, it can be easy to feel abandoned by Christians and even by God when you can no longer physically enter the church doors. It may seem that loneliness is your destiny.

The woman who lived in Nain also suffered several losses. She was probably still grieving over her husband's recent death; otherwise she may have remarried quickly as most widows did. Even though widowhood provided new legal independence, it also was a sure road to poverty, because generally women were expected to do unpaid work, only in the home. Women who did not remarry and who did not have extended family usually had to resort to begging or prostitution. This woman was still alone, and so the question of her future may have loomed large: What would happen to her and her son? And then she endured her son's crushing death.

When Jesus saw the widow walking alone, with her dead son following in the bier, he instantly understood the desperate, lonely future she faced without the love of her only son. Compassion overtook him: He wanted only for her tears to stop ("Don't cry," he said to her). Jesus broke several cultural and religious laws at once in order to reverse the laws of death for this widow and her only son. He interrupted a funeral, touched a bier (which would cause him to be considered "unclean" for a day), and probably overshadowed the corpse (causing a seven-day period of uncleanness).[5]

Jesus' deep empathy and concern for this woman he had never met, however, exceeded any thoughts he might have had about becoming ritually unclean or losing face among those who might judge him. The only compelling reason we have for Jesus resurrecting this woman's son was that he felt her pain. She did not ask for his help, as so many others did. Yet Jesus brought about a very rare resurrection—one of three recorded.

This story provides evidence that God has deep compassion for us, too, because Jesus is the perfect reflection of God (Hebrews 1:3; 2 Corinthians 4:4; Colossians 1:15). What Jesus did for the widow is what God longs to do for you. Jesus may not restore your losses fully, as he did not fully restore the widow of Nain's losses (she was still a widow). But he does have resurrection life for you, whether you can enter the church doors or not. Ask Jesus to help you see signs of his love today.

---

[5] Hyam Maccoby, *Ritual and Morality: The Ritual Purity System and Its Place in Jusaism*, 6.

Questions for Reflection/Discussion

1. Have you ever had the thought "God doesn't know what it's like to be me"? What, in the Gospel story, indicates that God does know what it's like to be a woman?

2. What cultural values in our society and churches make it difficult to show the compassion of Jesus for women who are profoundly alone, and/or have an isolating chronic illness?

3. What did you see in Jesus in the Gospel story that you may have not seen in him before? In this story, what does Jesus ("the radiance of God's glory and the exact representation of his being," Hebrews 1:3) reveal to you about who God is?

4. It is easy to feel frustrated when, like Betsy Mae, we or people we love do not get a "resurrection" of lost people and abilities. But consider how Christ-living-in-you ("the hope of glory," Colossians 1:27) might be a sign of resurrection and hope for you or a grieving, lonely woman.

Meditation for Healing

Find a place where you can relax. Invite the Holy Spirit to come close and to help you be aware of being in Jesus' presence. (Even if you don't *feel* Jesus' presence, go ahead and affirm that presence.) Meditate on how Jesus chooses you to be invited to an extravagant dinner party. He rejects those who are married, wealthy, and healthy (read Luke 14:15-24) and chooses instead "the poor, the crippled, the blind and the lame" (all likely unmarried due to widowhood, poverty and/or ill health). He chooses you because he loves you but especially because you have time for him and do not reject him. You are willing to be the longed-for "bride" of Jesus. Give him the time he wants to spend with you now, just being with him. You do not have to say a word.

Conclusion

Perhaps you have read through this book, or parts of it, and been pained to realize that you have been hurt by the church. Maybe you have accepted that your role at home and at worship is inferior to men's, because it seemed biblical and it worked. You belonged. But now the pain in your heart has surfaced. The healing has barely begun. What do you do now? Where do you turn? Perhaps you are married to someone who is very comfortable with the way things have been and would not be eager to hear about your hurts.

I found a very helpful and healing resource when I was just beginning to notice inequities in the church in 1989. It continues today in an organization called Christians for Biblical Equality (CBE). CBE can be found on the Internet at http://www.cbeinternational.org, or through a search for Christians for Biblical Equality. Resources on the CBE site include a section on egalitarian services. There you will find links for therapists, spiritual directors (people trained to help with personal spiritual growth), and churches. If there is no support located near you, an inquiry to someone closest to you may prove helpful. A church, therapist, or spiritual director may know someone in your area who can provide encouragement. There are also CBE chapters formed in various cities around the country, an annual conference, a journal (*Priscilla Papers*), and information about life-giving books to read to begin your journey (find more information on the CBE site).

CBE provided the only community I had when I first began to experience the pain of being treated as having inferior status in the church. It wasn't enough, but it was far better than believing I was completely alone in my experiences. Reading books also provided a community for me, as I hope reading this one has provided for you. You are not alone! Even though we may never meet in person, I do care about you or I would not have written this book.

Perhaps you wish you had never become aware of Jesus' law of love, because it seems there is nothing you can do about your situation. If you do not submit to your husband, for example, he may hurt you or your children emotionally and physically. You may feel overwhelmed at the thought of doing anything to change. Churches are sometimes, but not always, supportive of women in abusive marriages. One first step to find support might be to locate a therapist who specializes in domestic violence. (Not all therapists understand the dynamics of abusive relationships, and so finding one who specifically claims to have been trained in domestic violence is very important). It may seem imperative that this person is a Christian, but there may not be a Christian domestic violence therapist available, and your and your children's safety is the priority. A toll-free call to the National Domestic Violence Hotline may help you to start finding sources of support: 1-800-799-7233 (SAFE). Or if you are not ready for that, just begin by learning about the dynamics of domestic violence. A Web site such as Medline (currently at: http://www.nlm.nih.gov/medlineplus/domesticviolence.html) can help, as can reading the recommended books listed in this book, particularly *The Verbally Abusive Relationship* by Patricia Evans. For a more general book on abuse within Christian families, read *Mending the Soul: Understanding and Healing Abuse* by Steven Tracy.

Perhaps you have experienced some healing in your relationship with God through reading this book, but you are still outside the church. If you are not happy with this situation, you might consider the various churches where women experience fewer structural forms of discrimination. Here are some denominations that have verbalized and/or enacted a commitment to Jesus' law of love toward women: Evangelical Covenant Church, Episcopal/Anglican, Mennonite, Quaker, and of course, any local church that has made a commitment to egalitarianism for women (see the CBE website). It *is* possible to go to church and feel better when you leave than you did when you came.

I discovered this myself when—after three months of searching—I found the right community for me in a small Vineyard church in Vancouver, Canada.[1] I found a refreshing indifference to gender in this community, where each person was regarded according to his or her giftings and strengths, or even potential giftings. There was freedom to try, and freedom to fail. There were no sermons on wifely submission (except the one I myself gave, explaining the 1 Timothy 2 passage), and nothing about male headship. It was all about worshiping Jesus and trying to be better servants of Jesus through the Spirit's help. It wasn't perfect, but there was a willingness to listen and a sensitivity to justice issues. For example, I asked the pastor to switch Bible translations to an inclusive language version, and he did.

It can happen for you too! You can be part of a community of believers committed to Jesus' law of love.

---

[1] The Vineyard in the United States and Canada have both put out statements of support for women in pastoral ministry. At this point in time, however, the actual practice of women functioning in full leadership is still evolving.

Appendix A

Interpreting the Bible (or "Hermeneutics")

I had never even heard the word *hermeneutics* when I first began learning about Bible interpretation. It made sense that there would actually be guidelines for interpreting the Bible, and the very thought began to free me from some of the proof-texting I had allowed to form my theology.[1]

Below are some basic principles of biblical interpretation that may help you as you grapple with the issues presented in the previous chapters. I've listed some books to help you as well, though I recognize that these cost money. If that is an issue, as it is for many people, make use of libraries: a university or seminary library; a public library; your church's library; or your pastoral team's library, if they are willing to lend. Or, buy used books.

---

[1] Proof-texting is using one or more verses from the Bible, without understanding the context, to "prove" one's opinion.

Basic Principles of Biblical Interpretation

1. If you haven't already, begin to make a habit of reflecting on your own cultural and church context as well as on your personal values. As you read a passage in Scripture, ask yourself, "How are my context and values influencing my interpretation?" (If you need help "getting outside" your own culture in order to see it, ask a newcomer to your country how the people in his or her country tend to view the people in your country.)

2. Make up your mind to find out what a given text would have meant to the original hearers in their cultural context, instead of focusing on what it means for you right now within your own cultural setting. (That part is important, too, but first things first!)

Some cultural values were "givens" when the Bible was written—almost no one questioned these things. For instance, the lower status of women and the institution of slavery were rarely questioned in the Greco-Roman and Jewish contexts. Paul reflects his culture to some degree in these areas (this makes sense—Paul wasn't God!). Jesus, however (who *was* God!), consistently acted counterculturally in his interactions with others when it came to issues of justice and mercy.

A great place to start learning about Jewish and Greco-Roman culture is *The IVP Bible Background Commentary: Old Testament* (2000) and *The IVP Bible Background Commentary: New Testament* (1994). You can look up a verse or passage and get relevant cultural information in a paragraph or two.

3. Understand the type of literature (the genre) that any given book of the Bible represents. For example, the Proverbs are an example of "wisdom literature." Other cultures in the ancient Near East had similar types of writings. But proverbs are not meant to be directive; they describe probabilities in life. To read Proverbs as commands is to misread the biblical text. A good resource for finding out about the genres of the Bible is *How to Read the Bible for All Its Worth* (2003) by Gordon D. Fee and Douglas Stuart.

4. Read the verse in the context of the whole chapter, the whole chapter in the context of the whole book, and the whole book in the context of the whole Bible. It is important to understand why an entire book was written—what situations were being addressed and to whom. Good commentaries can help with this. There is an appendix in *How to Read the Bible for All Its Worth* (see number 3, above), addressing what makes a good commentary and listing some suggestions.

5. Learn the themes of the Bible. Understand what is repeated over and over again. This may seem a formidable task, but leaning on Jesus' assessment of the two most important commands in Scripture will put you in a good hermeneutical place: "'The most important one,' answered Jesus, 'is this: "Hear, O Israel: The Lord our God, the Lord is one. Love the Lord your God with all your heart and with all your soul and with all your mind and with all your strength." The second is this, "Love your neighbor as yourself." There is no commandment

greater than these'" (Mark 12:29-31). Jesus' loving acts, his sayings, and his parables—understood in the context of his agrarian culture—show us concretely what Jesus meant by "love."

6. Read obscure or controversial texts in light of the themes of the Bible. No doctrine should be based upon an isolated or unclear text. To give an example, one controversial text often used to buttress the subordination of women is 1 Corinthians 14:34. It says, "Women should remain silent in the churches. They are not allowed to speak, but must be in submission, as the law says." Curiously, the Law (the first five books of the Old Testament, or the Torah) says nothing of the kind. But the Talmud, or rabbinic commentary on the Old Testament does. Some scholars feel that this parenthetical passage must be an interpolation (something added in later), not only because of this obvious mistake, but because it does not seem to fit in well with the rest of the passage.[2] In any case, the passage is controversial, so should not be leaned upon for church practice—particularly since it contradicts Jesus' law of love.

In contrast, one theme in the Bible is that both men and women are to use their gifts and authority. For example, see Exodus 15:20; Judges 4:4; 2 Kings 22:14; 2 Chronicles 34:22; Esther 4:13-17; Proverbs 31; Micah 6:4; Luke 2:36-38; Luke 8:1-3; John 4; 1 Corinthians

---

[2] See, for example, Gordon D. Fee's *The First Epistle to the Corinthians* (Grand Rapids, Michigan: Eerdmans Publishing Company, 1987), 699-708.

11:5; Romans 16; Acts 2:17-18; Acts 16:11-15; Acts 18:18, 26; Acts 21:9; and Galatians 3:28.

Often we as readers do not realize that when Paul addresses "brothers" in the Greek it is understood that he means brothers *and* sisters (an inclusive language translation, such as the TNIV or the NRSV, corrects this misunderstanding). As a result, passages that address both men and women as human beings and full participants in the church are overlooked (for example Romans 12:1-7; Romans 15:14; 1 Corinthians 12—14; 2 Timothy 2:2; Hebrews 2:4).

Good hermeneutics and good theology mean basing your beliefs on what is repeated and clear in Scripture. Good hermeneutics and good theology square with biblical themes, particularly the law of love.

Appendix B

The Role of Culture in Commands toward Slaves and Women

Did you know that the very passages used to argue for women's subordination today were also used to support the institution of slavery in the nineteenth century? Until the mid-eighteenth century, virtually all Christians believed that the Bible endorsed slavery as an institution eternally established by God, much like hierarchical marriage is viewed by some today.[1] No one wrote books specifically supporting slavery, however, as it was a cultural "given." When a movement took hold among evangelical Christians to abolish slavery in the nineteenth century, a counter-movement arose and other evangelical Christians began to write books defending slavery from a biblical point of view.

---

[1] The information presented in Appendix B is derived and summarized from Kevin Giles's excellent book *The Trinity & Subordinationism: The Doctrine of God and the Contemporary Gender Debate* (Downers Grove, IL: InterVarsity Press, 2002). For a much more complete look at the history of the evangelical defense of slavery, see the last part of his book.

They used many seemingly clear texts from the Epistles to uphold the social evil of slavery (see Ephesians 6:5; Colossians 3:22; 1 Timothy 6:1; Titus 2:9-10; 1 Peter 2:18-21). They also appealed to a text in Genesis 9 where Ham, a son of Noah, was cursed by his father to be "lowest of slaves." Proslavery writers said that God initiated slavery through Noah's curse. Other appeals to Scripture included the fact that slavery was practiced by the patriarchs: Abraham (Genesis 12:5; 12:16; 14:14; 24:35); Joshua (Joshua 9:23); David (2 Samuel 8:2, 6); Solomon (1 Kings 9:20-21) and even Job (Job 1:15-17; 3:19; 4:18; 7:2; 31:13). They argued that the Ten Commandments, the moral law, refers to slavery twice (the fourth and tenth commandments in Exodus 20:1-17 and Deuteronomy 5:1-21).

Moreover, they said, Jesus used slaves in his parables many times. He encountered them, and yet said nothing about the institution that enslaved them. These pro-slavery evangelicals argued that Jesus must have therefore approved of slavery. First Timothy 6:1-3 even argues that Paul's words commanding slaves to "consider their masters worthy of full respect" are in essence Christ's words. In seven different letters, Paul commanded slaves to accept their station in life and be, essentially, good slaves. He often added that masters should be kind (1 Corinthians 7:20-21; Ephesians 6:5-9; Colossians 4:1; 1 Timothy 6:1-3; Titus 2:9-10; Philemon 1:10-18; 1 Peter 2:18-19).

Great Christian reformers and writers such as Martin Luther, John Calvin, and many Puritans interpreted these verses to slaves as ordering the social stratum. Evangelical colonial preachers Cotton Mather, George Whitfield, and Jonathan Edwards all owned slaves without a second thought.

There is, indeed, a lot of biblical evidence seemingly in support of slavery. Do you buy it? How do you know that slavery was only a cultural institution and not ordained by God through Noah's curse on Ham? After all, Paul himself gave commands to slaves! We know this is bad biblical interpretation because our culture has changed—brave, insightful, and Christlike people were willing to risk everything in order to change it. Their countercultural acts enabled us to see how slavery is antithetical to Jesus' law of love—a primary principle throughout the Bible culminating in Jesus' incarnation, healing ministry, sacrificial death, and resurrection.

In the twenty-first century, evangelicals have forgotten this history. We are very much at a crossroads for women in that some of the misogynist attitudes throughout social history have changed and are continuing to change. In North America, the shift from an agrarian culture to a technological culture has made it possible for men and women to work in the areas of their giftedness and to share parenting responsibilities. Yet this shift proves threatening to those men and women more comfortable with a hierarchical social structure, with men on top.[2] Hence, in the 1970s when the women's justice movement took full force, evangelicals began to publicly argue from the Bible for women's subordination to men in the church and at home.

For decades now, evangelical women and men have repeatedly heard about the respective roles of men and women, where women submit to and follow men. But evangelicals *now* believe firmly that slavery is wrong, and have even addressed ongoing issues of racism in our culture. Hence, we can look at a passage from Paul's letters and clearly "see" what he says to women and "not see" what he says to slaves, despite the fact that both the institutions of slavery and hierarchical marriage were simply that—cultural institutions based on the belief that some classes of people are inferior to others.

Take a look at the parallels between commands to women and the commands to slaves:

1. From Ephesians 6:5 and 5:22: "Slaves, obey your earthly masters with respect and fear, and with sincerity of heart, just as you would obey Christ," and

---

[2] Contemporary Christian women arguing for their own inferiority and subordination is an odd phenomenon. Some women take the stance that "submission is power," and seem to believe that they have a powerful role in their marriages due to their willingness to let their husbands make the decisions for the family. Some actually do have egalitarian marriages in practice (and may even have prominent roles in the church), even as they argue for female subordination in order to be "true to Scripture." Others are afraid to argue otherwise, as the cost of fighting the hierarchical system within their families and the church subculture is too high.

"Wives, submit to your own husbands as you do to the Lord."

2. From Colossians 3:22 and 3:18: "Slaves, obey your earthly masters in everything with sincerity of heart and reverence for the Lord," and "Wives, submit yourselves to your husbands, as is fitting in the Lord."

3. From Titus 2:9-10 and 2:4-5: "Teach slaves to be subject to their masters in everything, to try to please them, not to talk back to them...so that in every way they will make the teaching about God our Savior attractive," and "Urge the younger women...to be subject to their husbands, so that no one will malign the word of God."

4. From 1 Peter 2:18 and 3:1: "Slaves, in reverent fear of God submit yourselves to your masters, not only to those who are good and considerate, but also to those who are harsh," and "Wives, in the same way [as slaves] submit yourselves to your own husbands so that, if any of them do not believe the word, they may be won over without words by the behavior of their wives."

Did you find yourself tuning out the verses to slaves and honing in on the ones to wives? For more than 1,900 years, both the commands to slaves and the commands to wives were seen as timeless, cultureless truths, and they fit in perfectly with the hierarchical social structure that existed. Once slavery was abolished and the human rights of slaves began to be acknowledged, those verses began to seem absurdly inappropriate. Yet the command for the submission of wives is still seen as pertinent in many churches. Adherence to this command to wives (and to the belief in women not teaching men) is even a litmus test for whether or not a person truly believes the Bible to be the inspired word of God.

Why do many evangelicals today see the verses to wives as universal and not culturebound? For the same reason that evangelical slaveholders wrote biblical expositions on the godliness of slavery just when the abolitionist movement was taking hold: A change in the social order is difficult, especially when it seems one is losing power.[3]

Read Appendix C for a brief look at a key passage (1 Timothy 2:8-15) that some conservative evangelicals turn to as foundational for the argument that the apostles' commands to women are timeless and have nothing to do with culture.

---

[3] For a book addressing the dynamics of social change within the evangelical subculture today, see Julie Ingersoll, *Evangelical Christian Women: War Stories in the Gender Battles* (New York: NYU Press, 2003).

Appendix C

A Brief Look at 1 Timothy 2:8-15

Most evangelical women and girls have come across this passage at one time or another and inwardly cringed. It is a hurtful passage taken out of context, as it smacks of the age-old hatred of women based in "Eve's deception." This passage is also used to keep women "in their place" in the church and at home. Let's take a closer look, however, using the hermeneutical principles found in Appendix A.

If you have a Bible, look up 1 Timothy 2 and read it. Preferably, read the entire book. Go on to read 2 Timothy and Titus, together known as the "Pastoral Epistles" (or Letters), too, if you have the inclination. It won't do to "cut and paste" the passage here without the context of the entire letter.

Let's start by looking at our own culture in comparison with the culture of Paul and Timothy. What are some things we should be aware of about ourselves as Christians in the twenty-first century as we approach this chapter, this book, and all three Pastoral Epistles (1 and 2 Timothy and Titus)?

1. Today, we have the "Canon" of the Old and New Testaments, as well as the wisdom of the church councils and creeds. Paul, Timothy, Titus, and the other leaders and churches did not. They were generally operating on oral knowledge about Jesus passed down from apostles to churches; any "Scripture" Paul referred to was the Old Testament. Christianity was fragile then. Heresies had not been adequately refuted, and creeds and doctrine had not yet been written.

2. We expect that, in North America, boys *and* girls will be well-educated from infancy onward. Greco-Roman and Jewish cultures of the first century usually excluded women from learning in any formal way. So it was very easy for men in that time (Paul included, despite his Spirit-inspired efforts toward equality of status, as seen in Galatians 3:28) to see women as easily "deceived," because women were generally uneducated and illiterate. Paul also would have been taught, given his rabbinic training and the first-century Greco-Roman culture in which he lived, that women are inferior to men and are to be subordinate—and that this inferior status was ordained by God.[1]

3. It is difficult for us to imagine a popular, mainstream "goddess" religion in our day and time, much less Paul's, as all the major world religions today are fairly

---

[1] See Alvin John Schmidt, *Veiled and Silenced: How Culture Shaped Sexist Theology* (Macon, GA: Mercer University Press, 2000) for more background on the misogynist milieu that has existed throughout history.

patriarchal, at least culturally if not intrinsically. But Artemis of Ephesus was a popular Greek goddess when Paul wrote to Timothy. (Artemis's temple is even one of the Seven Wonders of the Ancient World.) Many followers of Christ in Ephesus may have converted from this religion. In Artemis's temple, male priests were castrated and women functioned as priests alongside the men.[2] One can speculate then that women converts in Ephesus may have had the unusual habit of saying what they thought, when they thought it, about spiritual matters.

Those cultural comparisons give us the background for looking more closely at the crisis situation that Paul addressed by letter ("epistle"), in the Ephesian church. Timothy, a young man (1 Timothy 4:12), was tempted to leave his position as shepherd of the Ephesian believing community (1:3) due to—presumably—the stress of trying to lead an erring and divisive group of people (1:6-7). Paul urges him to stay in order to "command certain persons not to teach false doctrines any longer....Some have departed from [a pure heart and a good conscience and a sincere faith] and have turned to meaningless talk. They want to be teachers of the law, but they do not know what they are talking about or what they so confidently affirm" (1:3, 6-7).

Paul takes an unusually authoritative stance in this crisis situation where false teaching threatened the simple gospel ("There is one God and one mediator between God and human beings, Christ Jesus, himself

---

[2] Strelan, Rick, *Paul, Artemis, and the Jews in Ephesus* (New York: Walter de Gruyter, 1996), 93.

human, who gave himself as a ransom for all people," 1 Timothy 2:5-6). Paul mentions teaching or uses different forms of the verb "to teach" many times (see 1 Timothy 1:3; 1:7; 1:10; 2:12; 4:1; 4:6; 4:11; 4:13, 4:16; 6:2-3) and refers to himself as "a true and faithful teacher of the Gentiles" (1 Timothy 2:7). Notably, he only mentions the Spirit twice in 1 Timothy (3:16; 4:1). In contrast, in Galatians (a book that is often called "The Magna Carta of Christian Freedom") Paul emphasizes the Spirit and the freedom from the yoke of the law that faith in Christ and the Spirit's presence bring (he mentions the Spirit seventeen times!). It is in the letter to the Galatians that Paul says, "There is neither Jew nor Gentile, neither slave nor free, neither male nor female, for you are all one in Christ Jesus" (3:28). The situation in the Galatian church, where believers were listening to legalistic teachers outside the church, was likely not as dire as it was in Ephesus. In Ephesus, the false teaching seemed to originate within the church (see Acts 20:17-35, especially verse 30), was demonic in origin (see 1 Timothy 1:19-20; 4:1; 5:15; 2 Timothy 2:25), and was overwhelming to young Timothy (note Paul's urgency of tone in his commands to Timothy in 1 Timothy 4:11-16; 5:20-22; 6:2b-5; 6:11-16; 6:20-21; 2 Timothy 1:6-9, 13-14; 2:15, 22-25). Paul needed to "lay down the law" for Timothy to bolster Timothy's ministry in Ephesus; for the Galatian church, Paul needed to "usher in the Spirit."

Now that we have a bit of the "bigger picture" of the church in Ephesus, we can hone in on the passage and verses that have been used to universally limit women's participation in Jesus' church. First Timothy 2:8-15 starts out with an address to men, expressing Paul's desire that they should pray without anger or arguing. This rather unusual request suggests that some of the men tended toward divisiveness, so the problem at Ephesus was not only with the women. Paul does focus on women, however, in addressing the problem of false teaching—particularly "younger widows" some of whom "already turned away to follow Satan"(1 Timothy 5:11-15; see also 2 Timothy 3:6-9).

In the 1 Timothy 2 passage, Paul turns immediately to address women (verse 9). The kinds of "dress" issues—wearing gold, pearls, and expensive clothes—indicate there were wealthy women in the church at Ephesus. It is quite possible these women hosted some of the churches in Ephesus (as there were likely many house churches, not just one), and therefore may have had considerable influence due to their wealth and previously acquired self-confidence in the cult of Artemis.

Paul then shifts focus from the women's dress to their attitudes (verse 10). He wants to see "good deeds" in place of an emphasis on physical appearance. Next, Paul looks at another aspect of women's attitudes, encouraging women to learn in "quietness" (versus the usual but less accurate translation, "silence") in 1 Timothy 2:11. They needed to accept—instead of argue against—correct teaching about Jesus, as they were "always learning but never able to come to a knowledge of the truth" (2 Timothy 3:7).[3]

There are several indications that Paul is simply addressing this particularly thorny situation, rather than making commands to all women, everywhere, for all time. The verb "I do not permit" in 1 Timothy 2:12 can also be translated "I am not permitting," which implies a particular setting, not a universal command.[4] Also in verse 12, the word Paul uses for "have authority" can have the implication "to domineer." This is the only time in the epistles he uses this particular word for authority, again implying that this is a unique situation and that Paul is not addressing women in all churches everywhere, throughout history.

A crucial bit of evidence is that Paul himself left Priscilla and Aquila in Ephesus (Acts 18:18-20) to help Timothy, whom they had met in Corinth (Acts 18:5). Ephesus is the very place where Priscilla and Aquila explained "the way of God more accurately" to Apollos (18:26). In 2 Timothy 4:19, we read that Paul instructs Timothy to greet Priscilla and Aquila, showing that they remained there teaching. Priscilla's being named first was even more unusual than it would be now, and so emphasized Priscilla's unique teaching ability and role, given

---

[3] See Gordon D. Fee's *1 and 2 Timothy, Titus* in the *New International Biblical Commentary* (Peabody, Massachusetts: Hendrickson Publishers, 2002), 70-77. Fee says that women were already allowed to learn in the churches, so the emphasis is probably not upon the women learning, but rather upon their attitudes as they learned.

[4] Gordon D. Fee, *1 and 2 Timothy, Titus* in the *New International Biblical Commentary*, 77.

that Luke points out her primary role with Apollos. There is also evidence in other Pauline letters that women were not at all "silent" in the churches. For example, they prophesied (Acts 21:9; 1 Corinthians 11:5). Gilbert Bilezekian notes that prophecy is always listed prior to teaching when Paul lists spiritual gifts (see Romans 12; 1 Corinthians 12:27-31; Ephesians 4), indicating greater importance, especially in 1 Corinthians 12, where gifts are listed numerically. He also notes that if there were a "ban for all time" on women teaching men, Paul would likely have mentioned such when he spoke of spiritual gifts.[5]

That said, however, it is verses 13 and 14 of 1 Timothy 2 to which some appeal in arguing that women should be subordinate to men. Paul points to Genesis 2 and 3, the creation accounts. Yet the author of Genesis gives no indication that there were roles established based on the created order, nor that Eve was to be subordinate to Adam. God told them both to "rule" (Genesis 1:28). Their "one flesh" union is emphasized rather than hierarchical social ordering (Genesis 2:18-25). The Hebrew word for "helper," a word describing Eve in Genesis 2:18, is also used multiple times to describe God's actions toward the Israelites (see Exodus 18:4; Deuteronomy 33:7, 26, 29; Psalm 33:20), and so if anything, indicates a superior rather than an inferior function. In fact, if sheer logic is used, one sees that Eve was apparently God's crowning achievement,

---

[5] Gilbert Bilezikian, *Beyond Sex Roles: What the Bible Says About a Woman's Place in Church and Family* (Grand Rapids, MI: Baker Book House, 1985).

as God started with the lowest forms of creation and moved up.

Paul negatively compares Eve (who was "deceived and became a sinner") to Adam ("who was not the one deceived") in 2:13-14. But neither the Genesis text nor Paul himself elsewhere supports this interpretation. It was prior to Eve's creation that Adam received from God the command about not eating the fruit, according to the text (Genesis 2:16-17). Eve was working with secondhand knowledge, as is further evidenced in that she added something—"nor shall you touch it"—to the command (Genesis 3:3). Given this, blaming Eve appears to be a cultural reflex, not justified by the reality reflected in the Genesis narratives. Paul himself, in Romans 5:12-21 and 1 Corinthians 15:21-22, points to Adam, not Eve, as the originator of sin.

In Paul's defense, there is a beautiful parallel that can be drawn between Paul and Eve in these letters, though it is not clear Paul himself intended it: [6]

Eve	**Paul**
"Deceived" (1 Timothy 2:14)	"Acted in ignorance and unbelief" (1 Timothy 1:13)
"Became a sinner" (1 Timothy 2:14)	"Once a blasphemer and a persecutor and a violent man" (1 Timothy 1:13)
First sinner (1 Timothy 2:14)	The "foremost" of sinners (1 Timothy 1:15 NRSV)

---

[6] I noticed this parallel when writing a sermon on this passage in my preaching and worship class at Regent College in 2002. I think I have seen it in one other book since, although I cannot recall the name.

Paul shows God's response to sinners like him (and, hence, Eve): "I was shown mercy....the grace of our Lord was poured out on me abundantly, along with the faith and love that are in Christ Jesus" (1 Timothy 1:13-14). In fact, Jesus "considered [Paul] trustworthy, appointing [Paul] to his service" (1 Timothy 1:12). Consider this: If Paul's sin did not stop Christ from choosing him as a coworker, would Eve's sin really stop Jesus from choosing all women for all time to teach or have authority over men?

Paul's last comment on women in this passage, regarding salvation through childbearing (2:15), has suffered a variety of interpretations in an attempt to square it with the gospel. We know that women are saved through faith in Christ, not through having children. Yet the verb Paul uses is the same one he uses in reference to spiritual salvation. It speaks of the desperation Paul felt to help Timothy save the floundering Ephesian church, as the younger widows who had not yet remarried were causing havoc (5:3-6; 5:11-15). Paul does eventually revert back to "faith, love and holiness" (2:15) with regard to the salvation of women, but adds "with propriety" at the end to underscore his point about women's behavior in the church.

Paul was interested in using any culturally sensible argument to stop the false teaching in Ephesus. His argument about women would have made sense to Timothy and bolstered Timothy's confidence in his ability to take control of the situation. This was Paul's aim—to get Timothy to restore order and a proper understanding of the gospel in the chaotic Ephesian church.

This is a very brief look at a controversial passage of Scripture, using the hermeneutical principles outlined in Appendix A. I have relied upon good scholarship, but also the interpretive "lens" of Jesus' law of love, a major theme in the Bible (see Matthew 7:12; Matthew 22:36-40; Mark 12:28-34; Romans 13:8-10; Galatians 5:14; Galatians 6:2). Love does not say that God created some humans to be inferior (in role or any other way) and subordinate to other humans, as we can see in Jesus' example. With that understanding, I have highlighted the impact of culture in Paul's arguments to Timothy, as their culture did say that some humans were inferior and subordinate (slaves and women).

As you must know by now, other lay people and scholars have studied the same passage and arrived at different conclusions, using a different interpretive lens. It is important, however, to make the effort to understand what the biblical writer meant and what the hearers would have understood. Then we can begin to explore how the text might apply to us.[7]

---

[7] For a more learned and comprehensive look at this passage, please see chapter 4 in Gordon D. Fee's *Gospel and Spirit: Issues in New Testament Hermeneutics* (Peabody, MA: Hedrickson Publishers, 1991).

Recommended Reading

Aldredge-Clanton, Jann. *In Whose Image? God and Gender.* Revised and expanded ed. New York: Crossroad Publishing Company, 2001.

Bilezikian, Gilbert. *Beyond Sex Roles: What the Bible Says About a Woman's Place in Church and Family.* 3d ed. Grand Rapids, MI: Baker Academic, 2006.

Calles Barger, Lilian. *Chasing Sophia: Reclaiming the Lost Wisdom of Jesus.* San Francisco, CA: Jossey-Bass, 2007.

Calles Barger, Lilian. *Eve's Revenge: Women and a Spirituality of the Body.* Grand Rapids, MI: Brazos Press, 2003.

Evans, Patricia. *The Verbally Abusive Relationship: How to Recognize It and How to Respond.* 2d ed. Avon, MA: Adams Media Corporation, 1996.

Fee, Gordon D. *Gospel and Spirit: Issues in New Testament Hermeneutics.* Peabody, MA: Hendrickson Publishers, 1991.

Fee, Gordon D. and Douglas Stuart. *How to Read the Bible for All Its Worth.* 3d ed. Grand Rapids, MI: Zondervan, 2003.

Giles, Kevin. *The Trinity & Subordinationism: The Doctrine of God and the Contemporary Gender Debate.* Downers Grove, IL: InterVarsity Press, 2002.

Grady, J. Lee. *10 Lies the Church Tells Women.* Lake Mary, FL: Charisma House, 2006.

Hoggard Creegan, Nicola and Christine D. Pohl. *Living on the Boundaries: Evanglical Women, Feminism, and the Theological Academy.* Downers Grove, IL: InterVarsity Press, 2005.

Ingersoll, Julie. *Evangelical Christian Women: War Stories in the Gender Battles.* New York: New York University Press, 2003.

Keener, Craig S. *The IVP Bible Background Commentary: New Testament* Downers Grove, IL: InterVarsity Press, 1994.

Schmidt, Alvin J. *Veiled and Silenced: How Culture Shaped Sexist Theology.* Macon, GA: Mercer University Press, 2000.

Smith, Paul. *Is It Okay to Call God "Mother"?: Considering the Feminine Face of God.* Peabody, MA: Hendrickson Publishers, 1993.

Stewart Van Leeuwen, Mary. *Gender & Grace: Love, Work, and Parenting in a Changing World.* Downers Grove, IL: InterVarsity Press, 1990.

Tracy, Steven R. *Mending the Soul: Understanding and Healing Abuse.* Grand Rapids, MI: Zondervan, 2005.

Walton, John H., Victor H. Matthews, and Mark W. Chavalas. *The IVP Bible Background Commentary: Old Testament.* Downers Grove, IL: InterVarsity Press, 2000.

Webb, William J. *Slaves, Women, & Homosexuals: Exploring the Hermeneutics of Cultural Analysis.* Downers Grove, IL: InterVarsity Press, 2001.

www.ingramcontent.com/pod-product-compliance
Lightning Source LLC
Chambersburg PA
CBHW062205080426
42734CB00010B/1803